# THE BEST PRACTICES OF SUCCESSFUL FINANCIAL ADVISORS

## FOCUS ON CLIENT RELATIONSHIPS AND LIFETIME FINANCIAL PLANNING AND YOU WILL HAVE LIFETIME CLIENTS

NEIL WOOD

A "Must Have" book for advisors that crave more success, life balance, stronger relationships and fewer hours in the office.

**Neil B. Wood ~ Neil Wood Consulting**
For Worldwide Speaking Engagements:
Neil@NeilWoodConsulting.com
781 264-3361

**Foreword by Rob Jolles**

Written by Neil Wood in 2005 and published as The Magic of Working Smarter

Revised in August 2014 at the bayside office of Neil Wood Consulting at the Optimist Island Resort in Hull, Massachusetts

Never get so busy making a living that you forget to make a life!

# Contents

# Foreword

As a professional speaker for twenty-two years, I've had the privilege to watch many speakers lecture on many topics. About ten years ago in a small town in Michigan, I heard a speaker deliver a message that I took to heart. That message centered around one simple quote that I have up on my wall to this day. It reads:

"We weren't put on this earth to make a living. We were put on this earth to make a difference."

Two simple sentences, but a complex message. Can a working professional—who is true to his clients and himself—achieve balance? That means working hard for your client, and working equally hard for your family. The beauty of Neil Wood's book is that he not only believes this, he will tell you how. His philosophy is if you work smarter, you can find this balance, and I agree. Working smarter. Let's assume for a moment that we all want to work smarter.

The question is how? Reading will help, coaching will help, and technology will help. I have another suggestion. I happen to believe that the best person to teach you how to work smarter is you. I'm a process man so I need a repeatable, predictable process when I go to work on something. I've always believed that when you have a process, you can measure what you are doing. When you can measure what you are doing, you can fix it. The book you are about to read will provide you with lessons learned by others that you can apply to your world. So, in order to learn the most you can from these lessons, let me suggest that you keep an eye on a few things. There are two phrases that I'd like you to watch for because they will help shape what Neil is about to teach you. I also want to make you aware of these two phrases because I never want you to say, or think them again. If you can commit to this, you truly will begin to work smarter.

## Phrase #1—"It wasn't my fault."

This is a phrase that I want you to view as offensive. Whenever you hear it, what you are really hearing is, "I'm a professional victim. Whatever challenge I am experiencing, I will repeat over and over again. I'll do this because I have learned nothing from the experience." Wisdom doesn't come from a life based solely on success or failure. It comes from a mixture of each, and a conscious knowledge of the lessons learned from both experiences. How can you work smarter if you have never made a mistake?

Successful people are not afraid to make mistakes. However, successful people rarely make the same mistake twice. This is because they are students of their own behaviors.

A great exercise that you can put yourself through is to go back and think of any recent experience personally or professionally that did not turn out the way you wished it had, and ask yourself, "What could I have done differently?" If the answer is "Nothing" you have failed your first test. I could care less about the percentage of fault; I simply want you to be able to articulate the lesson from your experience. If you do, you will be taking a huge step forward to working smarter.

# Phrase #2—"There's nothing I can do about it."

Really? Change is always an option. Back in the 80's, I worked for Xerox and was on the fast track to rise to a Senior Management position. The cost was high. I spent over 200 nights a year out on the road traveling for Xerox. I missed birthday parties, soccer games, and general life events. This was the price for success. When asked by my wife when the travel would end, I had no answer other than, "There's nothing I can do about it." The more I used that sad phrase, the easier it became to say. As a matter of fact, it became an easy crutch in my life, and it began to conveniently spill over to other aspects of my life. One day I woke up and said to myself, "There is always something I can do about it." Obviously my negotiation skills were not up to par, because when I went in to Xerox and told them I simply could not travel to the extent I was traveling, they had no answer and would not budge. I did. I prepared my letter of termination and left a job many would dream of having. It was and still is a wonderful company and I will bleed blue "X's" for the rest of my life. It was also the best decision I have ever made professionally. Don't lean on the useless phrase, "There is nothing I can do about it." You are in good company because we all fear change. If you don't like the way things are going, change them!

Open up your mind and look at the puzzle differently, and Neil Wood will help you to do just that in this book. The lessons contained in this book will help you to learn and grow. They will allow you to learn how others work through these challenges. These lessons will tell you about finding your path to combine what you love to do with the work you do. If you love what you are doing, and the way you are doing it, you will be content on the job and at home. You will also be taking significant steps to not just making a living, but making a difference. Enjoy the journey...

Robert L. Jolles
President, Jolles Associates, Inc.

Best Selling Author of The Way of the Road Warrior; Customer Centered Selling; How To Run Seminars & Workshops; How to Change Minds: The Art of Influence without Manipulation; and finally Mental Agility.

# Acknowledgements

The early years of my life were quite a challenge, but I was fortunate to meet some wonderful people along the way. They shared their time, kindness and advice with me to make the road of life much smoother. The initial years of my career were also challenging, but once again, I met some fantastic, gifted and kind people who taught me how to be more successful without working myself to death. My mission these days is to make a difference in the lives of my friends, clients and community, as others have done for me.

I want to share a heartfelt thanks to Connie and Herve Morisseau for welcoming me as their foster son when I was sixteen years old. As Rob stated in the Foreword, "If you don't like the way things are, then change them." I didn't like the negative and hostel home environment I was in while my father was away in Viet Nam, so I ran away from home at the age of 16. The

Morisseau family lived a few miles away and I was in high school with several of their sons. Marc Morisseau told Connie of my plight, my character, background and positive attitude and within a couple months, I was a member of their family. Their love, kindness and encouragement made the greatest difference in my life. I fondly remember Connie's words so often. "Babe, you can do anything you put your mind to. Work hard, be good to people and take care of your family and friends. Good things will happen." That was great advice to a kid, and remains good advice to any adult. Their children welcomed me as family from day one and I don't know how many other families would do that. Once again, I was very fortunate. Maybe God winked and I just happened to stay at "the Farm" while Connie and Herve vacationed in Paris. That event led to meeting Connie and the rest is great history.

I also want to thank Bob Wood (Woody), my amazing father, for teaching me early in my childhood that if you want to be a great athlete and competitor, you have to practice, believe in yourself and have a great attitude. That recipe for success also worked well in my career and life. What great lessons to learn as a kid! Dad wasn't around much when I was a kid because his career in the Navy brought him to the far parts of the world to protect the United States. He was one of the first Navy Seals in Viet Nam and was as tough as nails. I will be eternally grateful for the many memories amassed during his "free-time" leaves from the Navy and the time we enjoyed together playing sports, fishing and hunting. In 2013, he was diagnosed with cancer. The doctors gave him eight weeks to live with no hope at all for recovery, due to the amount of cancer from his knees to his lungs. It was his positive attitude and immense strength and will to succeed, which he continues to teach me that he's not only alive, but also happy and healthy today! We are thrilled to have him around to share more laughs and chats with. Like I said, he's as tough as nails and a great role model for courage. Thank you Dad!

You'll read about my friend Colonel Tom Kirk, who taught me so much about taking responsibility for my life, setting goals, sharing a positive attitude and focusing on my clients. Thanks to Tom, I stopped complaining and whining about growing up broke and started visualizing and working on a more successful future. In 1978, Tom lent me a Zig Ziglar cassette on Goals and success. That one little cassette was a game-changer for me. Of all the things I learned in high school, nothing comes close to what I learned on that cassette. The recipe for goal setting is simple, just like a combination on a lock is. But you have to know the correct order of the numbers, if you want to successfully operate the lock. Tom's gift unlocked my future and I still apply those lessons to my life today.

This book would not be in your hands without Mark Magnacca's friendship, encouragement, coaching advice and endless support. His "can-do" attitude opened my mind and created greater opportunities in my career. He encouraged me to work smarter during my sales career in financial services. He taught me how to design a personal biography page. That opened many closed doors for me because it was a simple way for prospects to learn about me first, notice our common interests and realize the valuable skills I could apply to help them grow their business. Mark also helped me create a personal introduction script for managers to utilize to introduce me to the audience before a presentation. That small paragraph set me apart from all other salespeople because it revealed my skills and background as a value added partner. Mark's skills at scripting and the importance of the right words at the right time improved my speaking skills and helped me land the best role of my career. Being hired by Jim Salners and AIM Investments for the National Speakers Bureau was a dream come true. I had enjoyed sales for years, but I LOVE being on stage teaching others how to create solid and long-lasting relationships with their clients and grow their businesses, gain more referrals and have more fun with clients they enjoy. The lessons I learned from Mark are priceless, and I achieve more progress each year.

Thank you also to the great sales managers who taught me so much about life, business, leadership and integrity. Tony Poleondakis, Tony Rogers, Pat Miller, Jim Salners, Mark Ryan and Bayard Closser are great role models and masters at their craft. I thank you all for teaching me how to be a more successful salesman, coach, keynote speaker and how to have more fun in my career and life.

Finally, thanks to my three children for being so darn patient with me while I have traveled throughout the United States as a sales rep and professional speaker. They are the highlight of my life. The best part of my day and life is sharing laughs and smiles with them. Everything else is a bonus. www.neilwoodconsulting.com

## The Warm-up to the Story

Tim Swift, an advisor with a prominent financial firm, was in his early forties. He was the type of guy you always enjoyed being around whether it was at the golf course, at the coffee shop, or at a neighbor's barbecue. He was the one who would ask questions and then actually listen to your answers, not because he was nosy but because he cared. He had a lot of buddies and a few close friends, but the pride and joy of his life was his family. He enjoyed and shared hours with his children who loved to play hockey, soccer, golf, and basketball and enjoyed the occasional snowboarding trip. He also had the good fortune of having two beautiful women in his life, his wife and young daughter. Life was good for the most part. Tim enjoyed helping people reach their financial goals and strengthen their financial lives, but he was at a crossroads and not sure what to do next.

He wanted to find a way to share more quality time with his family while they were still young, take more vacations, and not be so consumed by his career.

He had a successful career compared to many of his peers, but he constantly wondered how he could run his business more efficiently. Tim's positive attitude and willingness to go the extra mile with his clients assured his success. His mission statement included the commitment to providing service and an attention to clients that was far superior to that which his competitors offered. In theory, it was an outstanding way to run a business. In practice, however, it took a tremendous amount of time. Now that Tim had hundreds of clients, maintaining that "extra-mile" level of service had become overwhelming. The hours of focus and effort were wearing him down, affecting his generally good attitude, and taking the enjoyment out of his business. This was like a marathon with no finish line. He desperately wanted to find some balance in his life so that he could have more leisure time. Tim knew he had to make some drastic changes, so he called his good friend Mark. Tim and Mark had been close friends for ten years and gave each other advice when it was needed. Tim explained the things going on in his business, the number of hours required to maintain that "extra-mile" level of service, and some of his goals. One of his goals was to work just five days a week. He wanted to use the weekends to do something fun, like play golf or share quality time with his family, but right now, he couldn't without feeling guilty. It was impossible to take a day off, because he had so many clients relying on him.

Mark understood Tim's dilemma and, as a good friend, listened patiently. He sensed that Tim was ready to discover a better way to manage his business and his life. Mark admired his friend's dedication to his clients and career but also knew from experience that it would not be long before Tim burned out. Tim's energy would decline and that would affect his attitude toward and passion for the business. Mark personally knew this scenario all too well. He had been a top salesman in the financial planning business for many years while he used public seminars to build his business during the 1980s and 1990s. In the financial services industry, he was known as a "huge producer," which to the rest of us means a highly successful salesperson who makes a lot more money than most of his peers. He rose to the top 1% of all salespeople at his firm very quickly, despite being so young and looking even younger. Numerous newspaper articles raved of his success and his achievement awards, and included photos of him on golf outings with celebrities.

One day, he decided it was time to rethink his strategy in life. Although he was paid well and had a beautiful European sports car and a second home on the ocean, the work did not excite him anymore and money was not an issue in his life. When he analyzed which part of the business really excited him, he realized it was the client and prospect seminars that gave him great joy and energy. He looked forward to them more than anything else in his business. He was extremely competent and persuasive as a speaker. Anyone who watched him in action knew that speaking and explaining his ideas and concepts were his strengths. Eventually he sold his financial planning business in order to start a training business. Mark started training other advisors and sales reps who wanted to be more successful. He loved what he did and made more money than ever before. The transition took a couple of years but was well worth the challenges he faced initially. Mark compared life to a marathon. Some miles are easy, some are challenging, and others are downright ugly. But to complete the marathon, one has to persevere and keep the finish line in mind. It also helps to have a coach who has marathon experience.

Mark knew exactly what Tim needed and just the person who could help. He had a good friend who was a life coach and suggested Tim meet with her. "She's a life coach? What's that?" asked Tim.

"Tim, do you know how your clients come to you with their financial concerns and goals?"

"Yes, Mark, I do."

"Well, Kimberly acts as a career advisor to successful executives like you. She's been coaching for ten years, has written four books, and has plenty in common with you. You are both runners, successful in your careers, have endless energy and are very optimistic."

Tim had heard about coaches for business from one of his buddies ten years ago but did not have a chance to get more information. He had just been too busy to look into it back then, but now he was ready to make the time. Mark gave him Kimberly's number and promised to let her know that Tim would be calling soon. Mark sensed that this was a turning point in Tim's life.

It was a point many people faced in their careers, relationships, lifestyles, or fitness level, when they absolutely had to leave their comfort zones and make changes. Tim had no doubt that he could continue his lifestyle, but for his own sake, he had to make changes soon. Tim took Mark's advice and began to compare his life to a marathon, not a sprint. He often mentioned in his investment seminars that if we have a plan, the desire, and the discipline to do what is necessary, we would continually get closer to our goals and eventually reach them. Tim was ready to start a new marathon, so that he could reach his goal of having more time off to enjoy his personal life.

*He also compared life to a marathon, not a sprint. He often mentioned in his investment seminars that if we have a plan, the desire, and the discipline to do what is necessary, we would continually get closer to our goals and eventually reach them.*

## Chapter Recap:

Sometimes, we get into a rut or a slump or simply work far too hard. Working harder doesn't guarantee success. If you work fifty hours a week and someone else works seventy-five, they won't necessarily be fifty percent more successful. When I was a professional marathon runner in the 1980s, I often ran a hundred miles each week. Some of my competitors saw the success I was having and all the races I winning, so they decided to run ten to twenty miles more than I did each week. However, they didn't get better, they got injured and never did race well again. It was counterproductive to their goal. Work smarter and follow the lead of those who embrace the best practices of financial advisors, and not only be more successful but also a more fulfilled and happier person. I know of too many financial advisors who are wildly successful at work, but their home and personal life is pitiful and miserable.

Here is a terrific question to ask yourself regularly. "Is what I'm doing right now, the Best use of my time?" Prioritize your activities. Is my spouse, partner or family happy with the amount of time that I'm working? The secret to success is to find balance in life. Just because you are busy, does not mean you are making progress. Make the best use of your time at home, at work and when you are having fun. If you are having a problem with balance in your life, then reach out for help. It helps to have a friend or a coach to talk to about some of the challenges we are facing in life, get a different perspective and then make subtle changes in your life. The best athletes, salespeople, politicians, Hollywood celebrities and professional speakers hire coaches to help them reach the next level. You will learn something meaningful and useful by hiring someone to take a look at your business. You have nothing to lose and plenty to gain.

This book is written primarily for people who are running their own businesses and for anyone in sales, customer service and other businesses that thrive on repeat business from their customers. If you implement these practices regularly, you will find that they will also enrich your personal life. We live in a very competitive world, so outstanding customer service and client appreciation is vital to your success. Share the ideas that inspire you. My goal is to trigger new thoughts and ideas on how to find more balance in your life. We can learn so much from others if we are open to new and better ways.

# Chapter 1
# Meeting the Life Coach

Tim and Kimberly talked on Tuesday morning to set up a time to meet.

"Kimberly, I don't have much spare time right now, but I really want to talk with you. Mark speaks so highly of you, and I sure could use some coaching advice on how to manage my life better."

"Okay, Tim, would you prefer to meet for breakfast or lunch?"

"I would love to meet for either, but I'm in my office by 7:30 AM and stay until 6:00 PM. I usually eat at my desk or take clients to lunch to make the most of my day."

"Hmm," Kimberly replied. "It sounds like we need to meet soon. What do you do before going to the office?" Tim told her he goes for his morning run along the beach to get mentally ready for the day.

"Great, you like to run? I run every morning too. Let's meet for an early morning run and talk about your visit with our friend Mark."

Kimberly had started her own coaching business long before business coaching was popular. She was a sales rep for a pharmaceutical company during the 1970s and 1980s and made millions of dollars over the years. Most successful people will tell you that when you've made that much money in your career, it's not about the money anymore. Many successful people get to a point when they look at their lives and wonder whether they could do something more valuable for the world, for their lives, and for society in general. Kimberly hit that point in 1995. She was constantly hustling for business, outworking the competition, and trying to beat her sales record from the year before. She was the sales leader for five years straight. It wasn't because she had the best territory or the best products. She was at the top because she always had a plan and the discipline to follow it, and she was outstanding in developing client relationships. She also did something that many salespeople talk about but rarely do. She kept in touch regularly with her clients and prospects.

She outsourced to a company that sent cards, newsletters, and notes to her database, based upon her request. She also used SendOutCards to create personalized cards for her clients. This gave her time to stay focused on what she did best and enjoyed so much, which was meeting with clients. Every client and prospect received a birthday card. They also received cards on other special holidays like the Fourth of July, Thanksgiving, the New Year, and even the celebration of spring. Her clients were raving fans of hers, sang her praises, and sent referrals. Nobody was more committed to her employer than she was, and nobody worked harder. Kimberly's life changed when she enrolled in a professional coaching program for financially successful business people. This is when she learned how to work better, take time off without guilt, and enjoy more of her life. The coaching program had such a profound influence on her life, that she decided to start her own coaching business to help other professionals. That was in 1995. Since then, she's helped hundreds of other successful, driven, and overworked professionals improve their lives. That is what she is passionate about!

The next day at 5:30 AM, Tim and Kimberly met at the beach for their first run together.

"Tell me what's on your mind, Tim," said Kimberly.

"Well, I'm not sure what Mark told you, but I'm a financial advisor to about four-hundred clients, many of whom are considered high-net worth individuals with investable assets of at least a million dollars. I absolutely love my work and I enjoy helping people reach their goals. The challenge I face today is that I'm always at work, either mentally, physically, or both. I haven't taken a complete day off in at least seven years and I'm not sure a routine like that is healthy over the long run. No pun intended, Kimberly."

Kimberly asked him why he hadn't taken at least one full day off in seven years. Tim explained weekends were for catching up with sending thank-you notes and emails, planning for next week's appointments, and reviewing the previous week's appointments.

"Don't you need a little time for yourself?" asked Kimberly.

"Well, my morning run is my time for me. I get mentally charged up and relaxed at the same time. You know what I mean, Kimberly." They had run two miles already and were still cruising at a good pace.

"Tim, what determines the level of service you give to each client?"

"Each one deserves my very best commitment, so they all get treated with an equal amount of great care."

"Hmm, I see," said Kimberly. "Have you ever reviewed the amount of revenue that each client generates and considered a ranking system of an A, B, and C level?"

"That sounds like the Pareto Principle I read about many years ago, which involves the 80/20 rule. I've considered it, but sometimes I think it's easier to just give everyone great service instead of ranking my clients. I believe it's important to go the extra mile with each of them. I've made that a primary component of my business plan. Besides, what if I rank my clients and rarely talk to a C client, then they end up hitting the lottery or gaining a huge inheritance? I could potentially lose that business because I didn't keep in touch with that C client."

"Well, I guess you have a point, but there are slim odds they could hit the mega-millions jackpot. In the many years that you've been in this business, how many clients have hit the lottery?" gasped Kimberly who was now trying to keep up with the swift and driven forty-two-year-old runner as they breezed into mile four.

"Well, nobody has yet, but you never know," replied Tim.

Kimberly calmly offered this small piece of coaching advice.

"I know we only have another mile left, so here's something I would like you to consider. It may give you a little bit of well-deserved time off. The most successful salespeople and companies in the world apply the 80/20 Rule to their businesses so that they understand which clients should get different levels of service. Typically, 20 percent of your clients generate 80 percent of your revenues. Not every client requires or qualifies for the level of commitment that you are giving them. It's not a matter of treating some as if they are less important, Tim.

I know of some producers who classify their three tiers of service as good, better, and best. Of course the A, B, and C approach is the one used most often. But realistically, as you think about your clients, some need and deserve more of your time and some less. You only have so much time to dedicate to work, and you've already mentioned that you'd like some time to enjoy other priorities in your life, like your family and golf."

"Kimberly, I know you're right. It seems the clients who call me more often and are the most challenging to deal with, are my smallest clients. They can be such a hassle at times. But, I have built my business and reputation on going the extra mile with just about everything I do. That philosophy has worked well for many years, but now it is leading to burnout."

"Tim, we jumped right into your business issues and haven't talked about your goals yet. What do you want to accomplish by working with me? For example, if we were to meet two years from now for a morning run to talk about all the progress you've made in the previous twenty-four months, what would we need to accomplish for you to see this as a successful relationship?"

"Over the next two years, I would like to have my weekends totally free to have fun with my family, get my handicap back to single digits, feel like I am in control of my business instead of having it controlling me, and feel energized and enthusiastic again. To be totally honest with you, I would be thrilled to be able to golf with clients on Fridays again like I did years ago, which would give me four days in the office."

"Now we're getting somewhere, Tim. Several of those goals can be measured to accurately see your progress. It will be challenging to measure your energy and enthusiasm levels, but I believe you'll notice the difference if we can accomplish the other goals. I like the philosophy of going the extra mile. The only major challenge you'll face will be in the number of clients you can actually go the extra mile with. To reach your goals in the next two years, I believe you will need to reduce the size of your client base or create a team around you."

"These goals are really important to me, so I'll do whatever you suggest."

"If you don't change how you work your book of business, then your clients and troubles won't change either. If you always do what you have always done, then you will always get what you have always gotten."

"I agree with you, Kimberly. Where the heck do I start?"

"I'd like you to call my good friend Mark Magna when you're ready to con-sider making some slight changes in your business. He's a terrific friend, author, speaker, and a great business mind that simplified the Pareto Principle to help successful people like you. He speaks at seminars throughout the United States and Europe. Mark is one of the most impressive minds I have ever met. Tim, you will be amazed at what your future can look like after meeting with Mark."

"Okay, I'll gladly call him. My method of being a workaholic isn't working anymore. I want to have more fun in my business and share more time with my friends and family."

"There are a number of other ways I can help you as we move forward. Over the years, I've developed quite an interesting network of friends in various businesses. If it's okay with you, I would like to introduce you to as many of these people as you want to meet. All of them have unique strengths and abilities, which they have used to build their brands, businesses, and lives. It's a terrific group of people and I know they would get along great with you."

"Kimberly, that is just the boost I want. I'm so glad we've had this morning's run to get to know each other. I feel like this is the start of a brand new day, and I look forward to meeting your friends. Thanks for the run. Will I see you soon to brainstorm more?"

"Absolutely. Let's keep in touch every two weeks. I look forward to it."

As Tim drove back to his office, all he could do was smile. He had heard something many years ago that made sense once again. When the student is ready, the teacher will appear. Kimberly was just the spark he needed to make some positive changes in his life. Good things were going to happen from this point forward.

*"If we were to meet two years from now for a morning run to talk about all the progress you've made in the*

*previous twenty-four months, what would we need to accomplish for you to see this as a successful relationship?"*

# Chapter Recap:

My business coach asked a question that really opened my eyes and changed my thinking. One day he asked, "When was the last time you took a full day off to do things you love to do and didn't do any office work or anything related to your business?" It had been seven years since I had taken a full day off, because I believed that I had to do some work on my business every day. The problem with that routine is you never let your mind get recharged. Think about pumping weights or running hard every day. The muscles do not get any time to recover and as a result, you get injured or burned out or both. Your mind works in a similar fashion. From that day on, I took at least two days off every weekend. I did things with my family, played golf, went to the beach or cruised around on my boat. The results were amazing to me. I was invigorated and felt so good about going back to work on Monday. I had a better attitude, a greater level of energy and my passion for my work returned. Most of us are not saving lives, so it's one -hundred percent okay to take days off to renew our energy. Your energy, attitude, relationships and productivity all improve.

The Pareto Principle is one of the best principles you can apply to your business if you have dozens, hundreds or thousands of clients or customers. Generally, eighty percent of our business is from a mere twenty percent of our customers. So the big question here, is how well do you know your Top 20 percent? These are your Cash Cows! Get to know them well by creating a list of the twenty most important factoids about them.

By the way, we also tend to wear the same twenty percent of our clothes from our entire closet. The 80/20 Rule applies to many things in life, but if you have a business and are trying to please everyone, you are most likely working too hard. You can't please everyone, but make darn sure you take care of your most important clients. They are dedicated to you and expect the same in return.

# Chapter 2
# The 80/20 Rule and Who Is Generating Your Revenue

Tim called Mark a few days later.

"Hi, Mark. I'm Tim Swift, a new friend of Kimberly's. She says I might learn more about the 80/20 Rule from you in terms of managing my business and time."

"Hi, Tim. Kimberly did tell me you would be calling, and I would be glad to meet with you, but there is no way I'll run with you at the pace you gallop. Let's meet at Starbucks for breakfast this Friday morning, if that works for you."

"I don't run on Fridays, so that will be perfect." After Tim put the phone down, he started wondering what changes he would have to face in order to move his life in a more positive direction. His work schedule had been crazy for so long. He was worn out, which was affecting his relationships with his wife and children. He wasn't the happy-go- lucky guy he had been many years ago, and he was lacking that great level of confidence he once had. His peers probably didn't notice, but he knew it and didn't like it. It was time for a change. He wondered what the future would bring. He had been in such a comfort zone for so long that the thought of changing his routine made him anxious. How would his clients react to his new strategy? His wife would certainly welcome a change in his work habits. She was always there as a friend for him, supportive of his goals and determination. Things could only improve and just the thought of that life change made him feel better. There was hope but more importantly, there was a plan!

Tim and Mark met Friday morning at 6:00, at the local Starbucks. Knowing that Tim wanted to be in his office early, neither one of them wasted time after greeting each other.

"Tim, I spoke with Kimberly and have a good idea of the business challenges you're facing. I want you to know your challenge is very common for people with your level of experience and passion in this business. I also want to reassure you that usually a few small changes in a business strategy and daily habits provide results that many people in your predicament consider extraordinary. I like to view this as a tune-up for a high-performance racecar. Even a Ferrari needs a tune-up regularly, right?"

"Thank you for the encouragement, Mark, but I'm feeling more like a rusted-out junk car in need of a major overhaul right now."

"Tim, improving your situation is going to be easier than you think. Just out of curiosity, have you ever run a report on your clients to see how much revenue each one generates for your business?"

"Not recently, but my guess is that the revenue levels don't vary much, except for a few of my largest clients."

"Well Tim, tell me how you gained your top thirty clients and take a moment to tell me what they're like."

"Most of them came from the public seminars and cold calls I did in the beginning of my practice years ago. The average age of my clients is around sixty and they are mostly business owners."

Mark replied that it would be useful to (1) get a printout of the total assets for Tim's business, (2) calculate the revenues generated by all of his clients and (3) calculate exactly how much revenue each client generated as a percentage of that total amount. This was the first step in the process.

"Call me after your report is run and we'll meet for another Friday morning breakfast."

"Thanks Mark, I'll do all I can to get it done next week or maybe even this weekend," Tim said as enthusiastically as always.

"Tim, do us both a favor and don't do any work on Sunday. Use it as a play day to do something you enjoy. I know you like to work but, really, do something that just makes you feel relaxed, happy, and refreshed. You take Fridays off from your running schedule right?"

"Yes, I do."

"Why do you take a day off from running, even though you love it so much?" asked Mark.

"Well," Tim replied, "I run a lot and find that a day off helps my legs feel so much stronger the next day."

Mark suggested that taking a day off from work is just as important to give his mind a well-deserved break.

"Just try this for me and Kimberly, will you?"

"But Mark, what if a client calls me over the weekend because they need something?"

"What you do as a financial advisor is very important, and I'm sure your clients appreciate your dedication. But Tim, you are not saving lives. If someone needs anything on Sunday, I'll bet you a month of coffees it could wait until Monday."

"Taking a day off from work will be tough, but for you and Kimberly, I'll do my best and take Sunday as a play day with my children. Maybe my wife would enjoy some time away from the house, too."

"That sounds good, Tim," Mark replied with his gentle and sincere enthusiasm. "When you get back to your office and start the process of gathering the asset and revenue info, please call me with any questions. You're going to be amazed at what we discover about your business. Your dream of having a couple days off each week for yourself is soon going to be a reality. I want you to know that this process is not really about having days off. It's about working more efficiently, managing time better, and finding balance in your life. Kimberly and I want to help you reach your personal goals as well as your business goals."

Tim drove away thinking of how the meeting with Mark was such an effective use of his time. There was not the usual small talk or overload of information. Tim's first impression of Mark was very positive because the first project he'd been assigned was a simple step that he could accomplish easily. There were probably many more projects ahead of them, but taking them one step at a time was manageable. Excited to complete the first project, Tim began thinking about what he could do on Sunday with his family.

*"Your challenge is very common for people with your level of experience and passion in this business. I also want to reassure you that usually a few small changes in a business strategy and daily habits provide results that many people in your predicament consider extraordinary."*

# Chapter Recap:

When is the last time you took a very close look at your book of business? What do your clients have in common? Did you gain your best clients through acquisitions, referrals, cold calls, public seminars or Special Client Events? Who is giving you referrals regularly? Do you have an effective script when you ask clients for referrals? How are you thanking those who give you the referrals? Do you actually have a referral process?

Only twenty percent of financial advisors have a consistent referral process. The easiest group to get referrals from is within your top twenty percent of clients. But, to get referrals, you have to develop those clients into what I call, Raving Fans! These clients talk about you and rave about their relationship with you whenever they have the opportunity. They admire and respect you, want you to do well and know how committed you are to their financial success. You can replicate those clients by keeping in touch more often. I'll touch on that topic in a later chapter.

One of the best scripts I've used with my clients and I suggest you try it with yours is this. "Who else do you know, who I can help in the way I've helped you with your goals and business?" Tell them what your guidelines are when it comes to your ideal client. When I asked my top clients for referrals, I told them to think of other advisors like themselves. I wanted to work with advisors who had ten to twenty-five years in the business, were successful, appreciated strategic business relationships and value-added ideas, had a good attitude and cared deeply about their clients and doing the right thing for them. I wanted to partner with others that had a burning desire to succeed, had integrity and a good attitude.

In 1998 I hired Mark Magnacca to help me grow my business and to teach me how to work more efficiently and work fewer hours. I was making more money than ever in my life, but I wanted a life. Mark asked some very tough questions to gain more insight into what I was doing to manage and grow my book of business. I was so busy prospecting for new clients that I was overlooking the golden opportunities I had for referrals with my "A" clients. I found prospecting to be real fun because I like the challenge of the chase and discovering ways to turn a cold call into a new client. That was fun but it certainly was not the Best use of my time and talent. Mark taught me several simple new ways of building my business, a high impact referral system and within six months I was bringing in more business from my existing clients and new referrals. I also had a lot more free time to enjoy with my family and at the golf course.

I took this tried and true "Business Building" information and created my own "value-added" keynote presentations to share with advisors throughout North America. I could speak with authority on the success of these programs because I personally applied them to the client base within my territory. I knew these programs worked and was thrilled to share with others that wanted to learn how to strengthen client relationships. Each year I gave 150-200 keynote presentations and the feedback was tremendous from the advisors that implemented the ideas into their own business. We were all thrilled to be able to grow our business by working smarter, not harder, fewer hours not more and to find even more balance in our life. Win-Win!!

# Chapter 3
# Working in the Optimal Zone

The following Friday morning at Starbucks, Tim and Mark met to look at the report on total assets, revenue, and the amount generated by each client.

"Good morning, Tim! What did you find when you ran the report?" asked Mark.

"Well, I ran the numbers for my assets and total revenue, and detailed how much revenue each client generated. I must admit I'm a bit shocked by what I found. I had miscalculated when I was mentally analyzing my business. I also took another step, based on your suggestion last Friday: I reviewed my list of top clients based on revenue and wrote next to each name how they had become a client. I am a bit embarrassed to say that only a few came from my seminars and cold calls many years ago. Most came from referrals. The referrals, which were unsolicited, came from many of my best clients, the ones with whom I have the best relationships. Maybe you should check the numbers for me, Mark, because it looks like these fifty clients generate about 80 percent of my revenue. Most of the others do very little business with me anymore. I'm not sure why. I never actually noticed until I looked at this report. The assets they have with me, which made me consider them a top client, were placed many years ago. This is shocking. How could I have missed this with all the effort and time I put into my work?"

Mark nodded, paused to collect the right words, and comforted Tim with his calmness. "Tim, I've coached hundreds of top salespeople in the last twelve years, and I find a similar scenario in many cases. Sometimes we get so busy in our business that we fall into a trap of confusing activity with progress. That's why we started this business review and analysis. The next steps are easy, which is why Kimberly and I are so excited about your future. Remember what we talked about last week? The process of working hard is going to be replaced with the practice of working better and more strategically, which many of us refer to as working smart-er."

This awakening was a little disconcerting to Tim. He always took pride in working harder than anyone he had ever met. He always believed his hard work was responsible for his success. He wondered whether it was possible to work smarter but not as hard. Mark could see the puzzled look on Tim's face and wanted to put him at ease.

"Tim, I'm going to assume you run at a very fast pace when you train for a marathon. Kimberly said you were averaging about seven minutes per mile during your run together. Why do you run at that pace?"

"Well, Mark, it's the pace my heart-rate monitor dictates based on my heartbeat and fitness level. It's referred to as the optimal training zone by fitness experts."

"Tell me more," said a very intrigued Mark.

"Each individual's optimal training zone is different, but what it calculates is a pace or heartbeat that provides the best workout for that person. Running faster will create lactic acid in the muscles and cause fatigue. Running more slowly than the optimum pace just won't burn calories as effectively or provide that great runner's high that we love to get."

"I get it, Tim. What you are describing is very similar to using the 80/20 programs. It involves working more efficiently, not harder. There is also an optimal balance in our work efforts. Work too much and it could potentially lead to burnout, like running too hard. But, once you focus on the top 20 percent of your clients who generate the greatest amount of your revenue, then you have the foundation for your optimal business model. The more time you run in the optimal training zone, the better your results, right?"

"Yes, Mark, you understand it perfectly."

"Well, if you invest more time and attention in your top 20 percent clients, you'll notice over time that they will generate more revenue, give more referrals, and increase their assets with you. Then you don't need to spend nearly as much time with the other 80 percent of your clients." You can bring on a young partner to help build strong relationships and service the remaining 80 percent of your book of business.

Tim thought about this for a moment, and then smiled.

"This approach is like the runner's high I talked about, isn't it? But this is more like the businessperson's high. Let me be sure I understand this. If most of my effort and time is invested with the top 20 percent of my clients, it will result in more of what I really need, which is more time off for leisure, family, and friends?"

"Yes, Tim. Working with eighty to one hundred top clients instead of four hundred will give you a lot more free time."

"So, I can still go the extra mile with my clients who are most important to my business but I don't have to try to be everything to everybody in my book of business, right?

"Absolutely," said Mark. "You get it. I have worked with some advisors who proudly tell me that they have more than one thousand clients. I tell them that they may have one thousand customers, but they aren't all clients. A client is very different from a customer. The relationship with a client is so much deeper and stronger than it is with customers."

That puzzled look appeared again on Tim's face. "Mark, forgive me if it seems like I'm questioning you, but it sounds too easy, compared to what I've been doing and to what most of the people in the office do daily."

"Tim, it may be simple, but for most business owners it is not easy. For example, how difficult is it for you to run a seven-minute mile?"

"Not hard at all."

"But it's difficult for most people to run a mile in seven minutes. The optimal 'work zone' is just like cruising along the beach at your seven-minute-mile pace with your heart-rate monitor, which you can do for many miles. That's working in the optimal zone for the best success in business. Just out of curiosity again, do all runners train with a heart monitor?"

"No, Mark, most runners just run hard. If they're training for a marathon, they run hard and run thousands of miles. I've seen many of my buddies get injured or race poorly as a result of this training strategy. But they don't know better. Remember the phrase 'no pain, no gain'?"

"Yes, but that phrase is about thirty years old isn't it?"

"It is, but some people still buy into that philosophy. Besides, many runners don't want to spend a hundred dollars on a heart-rate monitor."

"If you think of what we are talking about here, and consider your work habits, the same philosophy applies. Most advisors work hard, instead of efficiently because they learned many years ago to just work hard. Although there are other ways to accomplish what they truly want in business, they work with blinders on. You are different, Tim. You are open-minded to other strategies and willing to work intelligently in order to reach your goals. I'd like to see you run your business like you run your miles. Work smarter and the results will be better. Remember, it's simple but it's not easy."

"Okay, I'm willing to try this. What do I do next with my new discovery?" Tim was revved and Mark knew he was a winner, as Kimberly had mentioned.

"Take this list of your top fifty clients and prepare a fact sheet on each one. You'll want to know the demographics of your client base in addition to the psychographics. Get a thorough understanding of who they are, what basic personality traits they have in common with one another as well as with you, what drives them to be so successful, what their values are, and how they learn. That makes a difference in how you present concepts or ideas to them. I also want you to notice what type of cars they drive, their family backgrounds, the sports they play or enjoy watching, and anything else unique that you learn about them. Notice the pictures they have in their offices or homes. Once you have this information, some of which is going to take time, I encourage you to create a one-page personal fact sheet for each of your top 20 percent. You can use the Excel review sheets on this disc and see the examples I've printed for you in this yellow hanging file folder. Once that's done, you'll have a very clear understanding as to the exact type of client you have now. This exercise will eventually help you reach the goals you spoke with Kimberly about. You'll have more time for yourself, your family, and your friends, because you'll eliminate the small clients from your book who are demanding so much of your time. You'll be running your business like a business. The business will not be running you."

"Mark, my clients are so different from one another with respect to their ages, interests, backgrounds, and values. So I am not sure this exercise will matter in my situation. My book of business is probably not like most of the other advisors you've worked with."

Mark paused, as he so often does to let the other person know he hears and acknowledges what they are saying. He had heard this comment dozens of times from other successful advisors, so he was not bothered by it.

"You're probably right. Just for the heck of it though, assume that you'll learn something positive from this exercise, just like the numerous other successful advisors I've worked with and continue to coach today. Would it be worth a few hours of your time?"

Tim was slightly embarrassed and immediately spoke up. "Mark, I'm really not questioning you, and I have to admit, I'm intrigued by all of this. In all the hours I've applied to my business, these concepts have never been raised before.

How quickly would you like this done?"

"This is your business, Tim. How quickly would you like to move forward? When we complete this, the quantum leap you will experience will be like running at a six-minute- per-mile pace, yet feeling as comfortable as you normally do at your current seven- minute pace. The 'advisor's high' you will enjoy is like nothing you've ever experienced, Tim. You'll see!"

"Thank you, Mark. What should I do when I get this done?" Tim was like a sprinter in the starting blocks. Mark realized that Tim had an inner drive that few people could ever understand or learn. His years as a coach and business consultant had taught him that coaches and parents can teach people many things in life, but drive, passion, and sincere enthusiasm are traits people either possess or do not. Tim was one of a special breed, and Mark just knew he would be successful at anything he was passionate about. He responded to Tim's question with a simple comment.

"When you complete this step, call me and we'll meet one more time. Then I'll introduce you to Nick Woody who will teach you how to strengthen relationships with your top twenty percent of your client base and increase the amount of assets and solutions they have with you. Our goal here is to help you gain more time with your family and friends while growing your business strategically. Keeping in touch with your best clients is critical to your future success, and Nick is an expert in that area. Keep plugging, Tim. You're doing great and I look forward to seeing you soon."

"Thank you so much for meeting with me, Mark. Are you sure you don't want to go for a run for our next meeting?"

"Tim, only if I can ride a bike alongside you. Your enthusiasm will be enough to keep me going for a long time!"

"Okay, see you soon, Mark."

*His years as a coach and business consultant taught him that coaches and parents can teach people many things in life, but drive, passion, and sincere enthusiasm are traits people either possess or do not.*

Tim thought about his time with Mark and became fascinated with the idea that more advisors did not follow this business model. He remembered a story Mark had shared with him during their coffee. Earlier in the week, Mark had met with a dozen financial advisors that worked for the local bank. They told him they wanted more very wealthy clients. Mark asked how often they met with and how well they knew their current high net worth clients. One of the reps told Mark, that of his top twenty wealthiest clients; there were ten he had never met face to face in the last year. When Mark asked the group how often they contacted their wealthiest clients, the average was once a year and a few said twice. Stunned by these answers, Mark asked what their most pressing concern was. The bank advisors wondered why many of these clients had advisors from other investment firms handling their investments even though they kept large sums of cash at the bank.

They actually had two major issues: they wanted more high-net-worth clients but they were not taking great care of the ones they already had. They were guilty of an issue known as benign neglect. They didn't mean any harm to their clients, but they took them for granted and didn't take the time to get to know them personally. These bank advisors were confusing customers with clients. Mark knew from his business experience that if you don't provide the services and attention the affluent want, they will take their business elsewhere. This is especially true after volatile markets. The more Tim thought about the advisors who complained, the more he realized that this business was not rocket science. Yet there were advisors all over the country that apparently overlooked their current clients because they became so focused on finding new ones. It reminded him of the story referred to as "Acres of Diamonds."

The Acres of Diamonds story is about a young man who lived on a farm. One day, he happened to speak with a traveler who shared a story about people in foreign lands who had struck it rich in diamonds and were now living the life of luxury. The farmer was frustrated and discontented by his lack of wealth, so he decided to sell his farm and venture worldwide in search of diamonds. After many years of searching through deserts, jungles, and mountains, he was still broke. Out of desperation, he took his own life. The man who bought his farm for a very modest amount was in the fields one day when he noticed a flash of light from a black stone in a shallow stream. Curious, the farmer pulled the stone from the shallow water and brought it to his home. A friend noticed the stone and realized that it was a diamond. The field turned out to be one of the largest diamond mines in history. The previous owner had left a property worth millions, in search of success and riches. He died broke and frustrated. The moral of the story, which really hit home for Tim, was simple: Sometimes we just need to look in our own back yard or in our own book of business to see the diamond mine. What is seemingly simple is not always that easy.

*I have worked with some advisors who proudly tell me that they have more than one thousand clients. I tell them that they may have one thousand customers, but they aren't all clients. A client is very different from a customer. The relationship with a client is so much deeper and stronger than it is with customers.*

*They were guilty of an issue known as benign neglect. They didn't mean any harm to their clients, but they took them for granted and didn't take the time to get to know them personally. These bank advisors were confusing customers with clients.*

## Chapter Recap:

How well do you know the top 20 percent of your client base? How was money handled when they were kids? What keeps them awake at night? What are their values? What motivates them? How strong and deep is your relationship with them? Do they trust you enough to give you a referral? Have you asked them how often they would like you to keep in touch and how? Some clients want to meet in person, others prefer to keep in touch with a phone call and some just want emails. You need to learn exactly what they want and then communicate with them at least a dozen times each year.

In the 1990s, I met with each of my top clients and asked them how often and how they wanted me to keep in touch. I was so surprised at the different replies but it was such useful information. I made sure I contacted them exactly as they requested. This is a relationship business now. It was more transactional in the 1980s and 1990s, but it's "high touch" now, so if you want to succeed and grow, you need to be better than the average advisor. These are the little things that make a big difference in life and business. Are you working too much or not enough? What's your optimal time for phone calls to prospects and clients, research of the markets you cover and client meetings? Is your life balanced between work, fun, important relationships and exercise? You need to focus on each of these areas to be successful, happy and healthy. You are old enough to realize that no matter how much money you have in the bank, if you lose your health, your life changes dramatically.

By the way, the meeting with the financial advisors in the bank is a true story. I was hired as a consultant by a very large bank in Charlotte, North Carolina. They were rapidly losing high net worth clients to other financial advisory firms but couldn't understand why. They wanted to find more affluent clients but they didn't take care of their own "acres of diamonds" until I pointed out the obvious. Their strategy changed immediately and over the next two years, their business grew exponentially. Don't become a victim of benign neglect like these advisors did before they got the wake-up call.

# Chapter 4
# Strengthening The Relationship Will Lead To Success

Several weeks later, Mark's phone rang with exciting news from Tim. He took Mark's advice and reviewed his client base and was astonished.

"Mark, you'll be surprised at what I've discovered so far about my best clients.

Remember how you asked me to look for common interests, values, background, and things like that?"

"Yes, Tim, what did you find?"

"They have so much more in common than I realized. It ranges from the cars they drive, to their interests in sports, to their personalities and attitudes toward life and others. Many of them play golf, like I do. It's really interesting to see how many of my favorite clients share my values. The few who have caused me distress and who never seem to be satisfied are the ones whose values I do not share."

"Wow, that is interesting, isn't it?" Mark was not surprised. It was exactly as he expected because he had seen these results so many times before. But he needed Tim to discover this through his own experience.

"I've also started the profile page you suggested. You probably have an email from me this morning that lists the twelve things I want to know about each of my clients. I don't have all the details yet but will complete it over the next several months as I meet with those clients."

"I do have your email, and this list is a good portion of the info you'll need to strengthen the personal and professional relationships with your clients. You'll be pleasantly surprised at their response when you call your clients on their birthdays and anniversaries. Very few advisors take the time to call their clients.

Knowing this info is so useful when you speak with your clients because you can talk about the things that are important to them. When you see an article about a client's favorite author, restaurant, or hobby, call that client to let him or her know about it. These are the little things that can make a big difference. Good work, Tim."

## Twelve Important Personal Matters to Know about Your Clients

1. Birthday

2. Anniversary

3. Family names and vital information

4. Schools they graduated from

5. Favorite restaurant

6. Favorite sports teams

7. Favorite authors, movies, books, and magazines

8. Activities and hobbies they enjoy

9. Vacation plans and their best vacation ever

10. The type of car they drive

11. The name of their CPA and attorney

12. Something unique about them that few people know.

The pieces of the puzzle were falling into place for Tim. He was making great progress so quickly, that it was time for the next step. The excitement level was increasing each day now and the momentum was building like waves at the ocean.

"Let's dig a little deeper now, Tim. Remember, most of the focus during the 1990s was to gain as many clients and assets as possible. The number of accounts was a mile wide but the relationship was only an inch deep. Since you are going to meet with your best clients soon, there are some additional questions I would like you to consider asking them, if you have not already. Their answers to these questions will reveal their values, fears, hopes, dreams, and concerns. My assistant sent you an email with the questions a few minutes ago."

"I have the email." Tim looked at the questions for a moment.

How did your parents handle money when you were young?

What worries you most about the future?

What issues keep you awake at night?

What do you see yourself doing when you retire?

Describe your ideal retirement in vivid detail.

If money were not an issue, what would you do in the next fifteen years?

How much money is enough?

What investments would you avoid as a matter of principle?

What would you like to leave for your children or grandchildren?

Do you want to leave a legacy?

"Let me talk about a few of these questions that involve more consultative selling and listening skills. When your clients and prospects answer these questions, it develops a trust that a transaction-based relationship will never get close to. They are sharing their innermost thoughts, fears and goals with you. These are conversations they usually share with their closest friend or significant other. When you ask questions such as these, the client realizes how compassionate and empathetic you are. Your relationship as their advisor is elevated to a much higher level and if you address their concerns, these clients can become yours for life."

"Mark, there are several pages of questions here. Are these first eight some of your favorites?"

"Yes, they are. These will help you get more involved in the Life-Planning part of your business. The relationships you have will be a mile deep instead of an inch deep."

"I like these questions. Thank you."

"You're welcome. Tim, you are ready for the next step. I would like you to visit with my friend Nick who will share the magic of treating your clients like gold and showing them how much you appreciate them."

"I don't think I mentioned this to you, but I do have and use ACT for my database. Is there a better program to use?"

*"When you ask questions such as these, the client realizes how compassionate and empathetic you are. Your relationship as their advisor is elevated to a much higher level and these clients can become yours for life."*

"Tim, it's terrific to know all you know about your clients, and it's another thing to have a system to consistently keep in touch with them. That's what the next step is. One of my favorite quotes goes like this: 'People don't care how much you know about them, until they know how much you care about them.' I learned that many years ago from a motivational speaker and found it to be incredibly accurate. I'll call Nick and let him know that you're ready for him. He returns from vacation next week. Please call him when you have time."

"Mark, I'm on a roll now. I'll call him Tuesday."

"I enjoy your enthusiasm. I'll leave a message with his sales assistant to let him know he should be expecting your call."

"Thanks, Mark. I could never thank you enough for all you've done for me so far."

"You're welcome. This is only the beginning, my friend. When you look back at this experience two years from now and see how far you've progressed, you will be very proud. The best way to thank me is for you to help someone else when they are in need. Practicing random acts of kindness just makes the world a better place."

"I'll gladly do it," Tim said sincerely.

Tim thought about his conversations with Mark as he ran along the beach.

This small change in his business model could provide just the boost he needed to reach both his personal and business goals. He was somewhat frustrated that it took so many years to learn something so simple, but he did not waste time worrying about the past. At least he knew it now, and he would implement it immediately.

*"Most of the focus during the 1990s was to gain as many clients and assets as possible. The number of accounts was a mile wide but the relationship was only an inch deep. Over the last fourteen years, the strength of the relationship with your clients has determined if they leave you for another advisor or they are your raving fans and referral source."*

## Chapter Recap:

Learn all you can about your clients, their interests and financial concerns, and those relationships will be nearly unbreakable for years to come. Keep your promises, be in touch a dozen times each year and take a personal interest in their life. If you do, then you'll know the answers to the twelve key points about your clients listed in the chapter. Those twelve important personal matters are critical to know, so if you don't know the answers to all of them yet, begin today by calling five clients each day to set up a meeting with them. You can't ask all the questions in one sitting because it will seem more like an interrogation, which is not very comfortable for either of you. But ask questions each time you talk with your client and you will soon have all the answers you need. I speak from experience. When I was a wholesaler calling on financial advisors in the 1990s, this is exactly what I did with my better and best clients. They were very loyal to me, despite the fact that the mutual funds at my company were not very competitive compared to the dozens of other mutual fund companies in my territory. My clients knew that I always returned their calls within three hours, kept my promises and was constantly sharing sales ideas to help them grow their practice.

The questions about how money was handled, their fears, how much money is enough etc., create deep and meaningful conversations that solidify your value as their advisor. You may feel some regret that you have not been asking these questions since you started in the financial services business, but part of life and success is learning new and better ways to succeed. It is not about the number of hours you put into the business. It is what you do with the hours while you are working on your business. There are more terrific books on Amazon that address consultative selling and excellent thought-provoking questions you need to ask your clients. Mitch Anthony has written several books on this topic and "Your Clients For Life" is excellent. He and Scott West also wrote Storyselling for Financial Advisors and it should be mandatory reading for most advisors who want to communicate more effectively with prospects and clients. Work smarter and you'll be more balanced and successful in your life!

# Chapter 5
# The Product Is You: Be a Solution Provider to All Your Clients' Needs

Tim thought about all he had learned the past few weeks. He had so much more clarity about his business and life now. A huge burden came off of his shoulders, and he knew he would be taking some pleasurable and guilt-free days off soon. He wondered how he had landed on this high-speed merry-go- round of working seven days a week. He could not remember the last day he did not do any business-related work. Then he remembered one of the top salesmen he had met early in his career who had told him that this is an eighty-hour-a- week business, filled with cold calls, rejection, and a lot of fast-paced action. "You have to be totally dedicated to this business and your clients if you want to be successful," said the seasoned stockbroker. "If you commit your life to this business, you can make so much money you'll be able to buy anything you desire."

Although this guy was on his fourth marriage, eighty pounds overweight, and a heavy smoker, he was a legend in the office. He was "The Guy" who generated more commissions than anyone in the history of the firm. Certainly, he knew what it took to be successful. He had started in this business in 1970 and quickly became a master at cold-calling techniques and public seminars. His suggestion of how to run a business had to be right because he was successful and had more than thirty years of experience. That conversation was at the beginning of Tim's career. At that time, he had no idea that there might be another way or perhaps a better way. It's the classic case of not knowing what you don't know.

Tim called Nick Woody as he promised Mark he would.

"Hi, Nick, this is Tim, one of Mark Magnacca's new friends. He suggested I call you to hear about your success with treating clients like gold and showing appreciation."

"Well, good morning, Tim. Mark told me that you would be calling me this morning. When would you like to meet?"

"My schedule finally has some flexibility in it Nick. I'm normally ready after my morning run and can meet around 7:00 AM."

"Oh that's right, you're the runner who likes to fly along the beach each morning, right?"

"Yes, it's such an energizing start to my day."

"I like to run also. Let's meet at the beach tomorrow morning at 5:30 AM. We can talk while we run, if that's okay with you."

"That works for me, Nick. But what do you look like?"

"My assistant sent my personal biography to your email address while we've been talking. My photo is on it with a few highlights of my background. I drive a gold-colored car with a license plate that reads WINWIN. I'll see you in the morning."

Tim was impressed with all the background Mark had given Nick. He knew his personal background and email address already. He opened the email, anxious to find out what he and Nick had in common. Nick's biography was brief but packed with interesting and impressive details. Nick was a runner, lived on the coast, graduated from the same college as Tim had, and also had three children. That was all good. What really impressed Tim was that Nick had spoken at more than five hundred events, was published in numerous magazines, and had written a book on how to run a better business and enjoy life. Tim felt like he knew him already just from a quick glance at his bio. This was only the second personal biography of someone, other than a portfolio manager, that Tim had seen since he had started in the business. It made a lot of sense for Nick to have a personal biography because he had years of experience and accomplishments to include in his bio. Tim thought maybe, after a few more years, he could also have a bio, so he made a mental note for his to-do list.

The next morning they met at the beach. Both of them were early, so they started running at quarter past five.

"So, Tim, how many years have you been running?"

"I started running in college about twenty-three years ago for peace of mind and fitness. It gives me so much energy and confidence. I don't know what I would do without it."

Nick agreed with him. "It is a great energy boost, isn't it? I've been running for twenty-five years now. Even though it started just as a jog, I set my goals, read about all the successful runners I could find articles on, and in time became fairly competitive at it. Our business can be operated in a similar way. Once we decide what we want to accomplish, all we need to find is that recipe for success that others have used. There's no need to reinvent the wheel, as they say."

"Nick, when I was fairly new in this business around eighteen years ago, I met the top producer at our firm who told me about the eighty hours of weekly commitment, cold calls, rejection, and hard work I would have to put in for many years, if I wanted to be successful like him. What do you think of his recipe for success?"

"That recipe worked well during the 1970s, 1980s, and 1990s, but like many things in life, there has been a transition to a better and more effective way to succeed in financial services and other businesses as well. The previous method of building a business really involved cold calls and pushing stocks, limited partnerships, mutual funds, bonds, and variable annuities to anyone who would listen. Every broker thought he had the best product on the street. But after the explosion of new mutual funds during the 1990s, the funds simply became commodities. There were more than 10,000 mutual funds at the time. Heck, if you looked up at the sky tonight, there are not even 10,000 stars visible to the human eye! Tim, think about this, if there are 6,000 growth funds all buying stocks from the same markets, how different can the funds be? If you look at the average annual returns for the five- to ten-year periods, the results of the top twenty-five percent are nearly identical."

"Okay. I'm with you. What should an advisor do now? How do I build from here? What's the new recipe for success?" Tim was determined to work smarter and more efficiently, so that he could enjoy time with his family and golfing buddies.

"Tim, our business is not about commodities anymore. Any product you can provide can be bought from one thousand other advisors within the state or through a 1-800 number. The most successful advisors in our business today focus on the one thing they can influence and control, which is the relationship. And it starts with knowing what the best product is that you have to market today. That product is YOU!" Tim thought about Nick's comments for a couple hundred yards.

"I've never even thought about our business that way. But, Nick, you know that I get paid for the products I sell and the assets I accumulate. Those are the two primary components that I'm measured on."

"I know. Let's take one step back. You can't sell anything until you have a client, right?" "That's right."

"Okay, so as you mentally review the list of the best clients you have gained in the last fifteen years, why did they agree to become a client of yours? Was it your firm or the funds it provided that wowed them? Or did they become a client because they liked you and felt like they could trust you?"

"Tim, our business is not about commodities anymore. The most successful advisors in our business today focus on the one thing they can influence and control, and that one thing is the relationship."

Tim was getting the runner's high as they cruised along the beach into their third mile. This new way of thinking about building a business was becoming so clear to him now. He said, "As I think about my favorite clients, it had very little to do with my company or the products we have available. Granted, I did need to have relatively competitive products, but nobody ever asked if this was the number one product in the United States. Most of them have even mentioned that they like me and trust that I will do the necessary research for their portfolio. They think of me as their friend and believe that I will do the right thing to help them reach their financial goals."

Nick emphasized what he had said before. "The best product you have is you. People will either warm up to you, or they will not. That's the first step. Once they trust you, only then can you begin to talk about the solutions you have to their issues and goals. Some of the most successful advisors I have worked with provide as many as eight different solutions to the majority of their clients. Life insurance, wills, trusts, estate planning, college funding, mortgages, long-term care, and wealth management are just a few of the solutions they provide. When an advisor provides that many solutions to their clients, it is very difficult for the competition to pry clients away. One advisor I know refers to this as 'owning the household' because he is so entrenched in the long-term relationship with his clients. This leads to more referrals and of course more of your clients' assets. Our business is about relationships, solutions, and mutual benefits. But relationships are the foundation to success in this business. It's not about stocks, mutual funds, or beta coefficients."

"This is quite contrary to what I've been hearing in all my years in the business here. It makes so much sense. What about the veteran in my office though? He generated huge commissions years ago and knows very little about his clients. He's never even met some of them."

"That was the old model, Tim. Those advisors are dinosaurs now. The transactional method of doing business is close to death. People's attitudes have changed over time. Investors do not want to buy things over the phone from a stranger anymore because so many investors lost money during the 1980s and 1990s. They bought stocks over the phone from strangers who rarely called them again. They want a relationship with someone they trust. I was at a focus group in the city yesterday with one of the most trusted research groups in the country. They interviewed seven hundred of the most affluent investors in the country over the last twelve months. Seventy-seven percent of these people, who have a net worth of between two and twenty million dollars, want a Wealth Manager. They want to work with someone who can provide solutions, not products, for the financial situations they are concerned about. They want to work with an advisor that takes a holistic approach to the client relationship and can help with all aspects of their financial life, such as long-term care, aging parents, college funding, mortgages, life insurance, etc. The funds and stocks are important but secondary to the relationship and the solutions."

"I understand completely. My veteran broker buddy moans daily about how tough the business is and how it's not like the old days. He's not a top producer anymore and rarely adds new clients. I believe what you are saying."

"We've already run five miles. Can you go a few more?"

"I'm with you, Nick. Let's go!"

"Tim, the next step I'd suggest is to organize your first client-appreciation event."

"Oh, I heard about these public seminars from the older advisor who used to be the top producer in our office. I did a lot of those when I was first building my business."

*The best product you have is you. People will either warm up to you or they will not. That's the first step. Once they trust you, only then can you begin to talk about the solutions you have to their issues and goals.*

"Actually Tim, we don't do public seminars anymore. I'm talking about inviting some of your best and favorite clients to a nice restaurant or an event that's fun."

"But they're already clients. I want to find more clients who are like my top 20 percent."

"You sure do. So Tim, tell me which method you think would be the most effective way to gain those new clients and to work fewer hours each week. The first way is to offer a public seminar to a roomful of strangers who are probably attending the event for the free food. We refer to these prospects as seagulls because they swoop in for food and then fly away, leaving nothing of any value to you. Or, you could show how much you appreciate your current clients by hosting a dinner or an interesting event to show your appreciation and strengthen your current relationships. You could also thank them in person for the referrals they've shared with you in the last five, ten, and fifteen years. By the way, do you ask for referrals?"

"Um, well, sometimes. Actually, I am really uncomfortable asking for them because I don't want to put my clients on the spot."

"I hear that all the time. So let's talk about showing your appreciation to your favorite and most lucrative clients and see how many will send referrals without you even asking for them. If you want to organize a client event, I'll e-mail the Ten Tips for Successful Events to you and have my sales assistant send my twenty-minute audio CD. For now, I'll tell you how they work. Have you ever eaten at The Capital Grill?"

"Oh sure Nick, it's a great restaurant!"

"Well, they have a private room toward the back of the restaurant that can seat twenty-five people comfortably. Call five to ten of your best clients who live within a thirty-minute drive. Let them know you are hosting a private dinner for some of your favorite clients at The Capital Grill, on the date that you arrange with the restaurant. Tell them this is just a fun evening, you're not selling anything, and you'd just like your clients to meet each other over dinner and enjoy themselves. Also let them know that if they want to bring another couple with them, they are welcome to, but it is absolutely not mandatory. Some people prefer to sit with at least one couple they know at dinner. If they are bringing someone, they should tell you so you have enough room and can arrange to seat them together. That evening, you should thank everyone for joining you for dinner. Let them know how much you appreciate their business and friendship. Then, you could introduce your clients to each other and say something interesting about him or her. You will be fascinated to see how many of them have something in common. It doesn't take very long before you hear all of them talking together. It's really fun to hear. If you want to give a brief market overview while they eat dinner, it's usually a good idea to talk for fifteen to twenty minutes. This is an ideal way to show everyone how friendly, knowledgeable, professional and articulate you are."

"That's a great idea."

"Here's the most successful way to wrap the evening up. Thank everyone for making the dinner such a wonderful event. Tell them you're glad so many of them have so much in common and you really enjoy working with them. Here's a script for you to gain more referrals. Say something like this: 'I want to thank all of you for being such a pleasure to work with. I also want to thank so many of you for the referrals you have shared with me in the past twelve months. This has been my best year ever for referrals. That's the best compliment you can give me, and I look forward to working with more people like you. Thank you so much.' What do you think the reaction will be?"

"Well, for the clients who have given me referrals, they'll be proud and feel appreciated. The clients who have not thought about giving a referral will probably start thinking of referrals they could give me."

"Exactly. This is a subtle and indirect way to get the referrals you want. It works like a charm every time. This type of event can be organized within four weeks, costs very little, is a highly effective way to show appreciation, and can be done for most of your top clients that live in the local area. If costs are of any concern, you could always call your favorite mutual fund or annuity wholesaler to see if they will help with the costs. Here's the best part. Instead of meeting with each of these clients individually, which is very time-consuming, you touch all of them at once during a two-hour event. Since I know you like to go the extra mile with your clients, you would probably enjoy this idea too. Take a photo of each client with his or her friends at this event and have it framed, then send it to them with a nice note. That picture reminds everyone of your special event and leads to potential referrals when their friends or family visit. I've already saved you hours of office work so that you can play more golf and share quality time with your family."

"Thanks, Nick. Can we walk the last quarter-mile to warm down? That's one of the best eight-mile runs I've had in years. I appreciate your time, ideas, and enthusiasm. Will you send the ten tips for successful events to me?"

"Sure, do you want it in print or would you rather listen to a CD while you drive to appointments?"

"Both would be helpful, if you don't mind."

"You'll have them by tomorrow morning. Is there anything else I can do for you?" Nick always closed his appointments with that question because it showed he cared and the response was usually interesting.

"You've given me so many ideas during this run that it will take a while to digest and implement each of them. I have a feeling my personal life and business will be perfect after I implement all I've learned this month."

"Tim, remember how it was when you first started running? You made progress and became stronger and faster over months and years of dedication and discipline. Be patient with yourself. We don't measure perfection; we measure our progress. Life as well as business is an ongoing journey with no finish line. You have so many wonderful resources, thanks to Kimberly. Call any of us when you need any clarification or just a good listener. We're in the helping and solution business, just like you are."

"Thanks again, Nick. I'll keep that in mind and keep in touch along the way."

*"They interviewed seven hundred of the most affluent investors in the country over the last twelve months. Seventy-seven percent of these people, who have a net worth of between two and twenty million dollars, want a Wealth Manager. They want to work with someone who can provide solutions, not products, for the financial situations they are concerned about. They want to work with an advisor that takes a holistic approach to the client relationship and can help with all aspects of their financial life, such as long-term care, aging parents, college funding, mortgages, life insurance, etc. The funds and stocks are important but secondary to the relationship and the solutions."*

A few days later, during yet another morning run, Tim remembered an old associate in Scottsdale, who had mentioned client events to him nearly seven years ago. The idea hadn't clicked with him at the time, but it made sense now, so he decided to give her a call. Her business was off the charts and she was consistently among the top 10 percent in sales at her firm.

"Hi Louise, this is Tim Swift. How have you been?"

"Life is good, business is good, and we're enjoying another sunny day here in

Scottsdale. What's going on with you, my friend?"

"I've been on a great adventure these days. I'm working with a business and life coach, which has been quite an eye-opener for me. I just learned more about client events and had this great urge to call you because you've been hosting these for years. Would you share a few minutes and tell me about your experiences?"

"Sure, Tim. I've been involved in more client events than I can count, but the total is probably around two hundred. When I see how successful these are and how happy the clients are to be personally invited by me, I am just fascinated at the relatively small number of advisors who host these events. I'm not talking about the old public seminars we did years ago, which were akin to shotgun marketing. I'm talking about events with a targeted group of current clients at each one. Here's the success recipe that works for me. Invite your most enthusiastic fans within your top 20 percent. Also invite some of your B and C clients who don't provide much revenue but do send good referrals to you.

I've seen the most success with events that have a total of fifty people or fewer. It's a comfortable size for people to mingle and ask questions without feeling intimidated by the size of the audience and they are much easier for you to organize. Try one this quarter and you'll see how successful they are. You'll get thank-you notes from many of those who attend your thank-you dinner. Now that's cool!"

"My greatest fear is that many of them will start complaining about the bad performance of the recent markets."

"Tim, these folks believe in you, they appreciate the fact that you invited them out to a nice event, and they know that the financial markets are not in your control. They have shared their dreams, goals, and hopes with you, knowing you will do your best to help them get there because you care. Remember, we are in the solutions and relationship business these days. While that wasn't the case when we started many years ago, it certainly is the strength of our business today. If they are still working with you today, after the last stock-market correction, then it's safe to assume they trust and believe in you."

"Thanks, Louise. That's exactly what I needed to hear"

"Go for it. Promise me you'll call with the good news after your first one."

"Consider it done. Thank you!"

*"We don't measure perfection; we measure our progress."*

# Chapter Recap:

The Product Is You is a terrific book by my great friend, Mark Magnacca. His premise is that the reason people do business with you has very little to do with performance, the company you represent or average annual returns. They do business with you because they trust you to help them reach their goals in life. If you missed this quote in this chapter, please go back to the beginning and read it once again. Yes, it's THAT important. "Tim, our business is not about commodities anymore. The most successful advisors in our business today focus on the one thing they can influence and control, and that one thing is the relationship." Read books about or listen to speakers who have mastered Lifetime Financial Planning. The best of them are excellent in communications. By that I mean, they ask terrific probing questions and then they listen to one hundred percent of the answers. If you do that, you'll be ahead of at least seventy percent of your competition.

I talk more about client events in Chapter 11, but it's worth mentioning at least twice in this book. I have been the guest speaker at more than two hundred client events, so I know what works for the audience and what does not. The ideal size for these events is about fifty people, but a dozen clients at an event works quite well also. I would not host an event with more than fifty people because people will not bond as well. It's also time consuming to organize larger events while you are trying to run your business. Think about how you feel when you attend a party. If there are 20-50 people there, you can easily meet plenty of people, have a variety of conversations and actually hear each other. The larger the party, the less intimate and the louder it gets. Keep your events smaller, host plenty of them and your clients and guests will enjoy themselves every time.

A client hired me to attend their large annual client event they were hosting, so that I could observe and then share my expertise in a review the following week. There were five hundred people at this event, an open bar and a very heavy meal served. Three hours after the event started, a portfolio manager gave a 60-minute presentation about beta coefficients and how he selects stocks for his portfolio. He was brilliant but the event ran too long, people were falling asleep in their chairs and in my opinion, it was a nightmare. I'd encourage you to host ten events with ten to twenty clients, include their spouse or significant other, and ask if they would like to bring a guest or two.

Welcoming your clients to bring guests serves two purposes. Your client(s) will have a friend to sit with at the event and you have the opportunity to gain a new client. My script for asking clients to bring a guest is simple and welcoming. As you call each client to see if they can make the event you have scheduled, they'll say either Yes, No or Maybe. For those who say yes, try this script. "Mrs. Jones, if you would like to bring a guest or two to the client event, please feel welcome to have them join us. Some of our clients enjoy having a friend with them, but it's certainly not mandatory. Just let us know how many guests you want to bring, so that we can be sure to have enough room and food."

That script works well every time. The script I would NOT use is one I overheard while I was in an office. The young advisor called a client and said, "If you would like to attend our client event, you MUST bring two other couples." I couldn't believe my ears. If I were his client, I'd probably say, "Thanks for the invite, but I can't make it. I can treat myself to dinner. Good luck and good bye!"

Clients events are so easy to organize and are always successful, if you follow my simple 10 Step Client Event process. How do I measure the success of a client event? You will receive plenty of positive comments immediately after the event and thank you notes the following week. Most people want to feel appreciated and that's one of the many benefits of a client event. You should also begin to receive more referrals and personal introductions from the guests you invited to your event.

## The 10 Step Client Event Process

### Ten Tips for Client Events

A client luncheon, dinner or other event, can be organized within four weeks if you follow this checklist. Planning eight-twelve weeks ahead however, will produce a better success rate for the number of people that say yes. This is the exact repeatable process I have used when I have coached top salespeople and helped them coordinate the 250 events I have personally been involved with.

1. <u>Location</u>: If you are hosting a meal, schedule a lunch or dinner at a nice restaurant with a private room. It should be a place that is easy to find, with plenty of parking, good food, and room for your guests. We have found the ideal group size is between twenty-five and fifty people, which will keep this intimate and comfortable for your guests. That is why a nice restaurant that is easy to get to can really set the stage for a successful event. Some advisors host a dinner at their home with great success.

2. <u>Speaker and Date</u>: If you decide to have a guest speaker talk during dinner...and the talk should be during the meal, find a very good speaker who will provide the presentation you need for the current market or a timely topic your clients would enjoy hearing about. This should be a brief, twenty to thirty-minute entertaining presentation, not a product pitch. Remember, this is an appreciation event, not a product-pushing night. If your speaker is outstanding, this event will be very enjoyable. If your clients have fun, business and referrals will often follow. Every time I have spoken at these

events, the advisor has gained more business immediately following the event. So find a terrific speaker with an interesting topic and expect to have some fun.

3. <u>Coordinate Available Dates and Times</u>: Make sure to check with the restaurant and your favorite speaker about their availabilities. Be sure that you have seen them speak to an audience before and know what the presentation will be. This is your event and you get the final say. Don't assume anything. Pay attention to detail. Believe me, I've learned from experience so that you don't need to.

4. <u>Financing</u>: If you do not want to cover the entire costs of the event, call your favorite wholesalers and ask if they will contribute to the cost, if that is okay with your company and compliance. Our business is about partnerships between you, your clients, and the wholesalers who sincerely take an interest in your success. These events are not expensive and generally one or two wholesalers can cover the costs. If you are going to ask for wholesaler support, only ask those you give business to. This is a WIN-WIN relationship.

5. <u>Invitation List</u>: Your goal is to have between twenty-five to fifty people at dinner or whatever event you are hosting. If it's a fly-fishing event or a short game clinic at a golf course, the number of attendees should be a dozen or so. Clients, significant others, and guests combine for that total. List the clients within thirty minutes of the restaurant. Then, call them...yes...call to invite them to your client-appreciation event. This is an important difference from the way most people organized events like these in the past. Tell them that you are having a small gathering of some of your local clients and guests and would like them to join you for a nice dinner or whatever your event is. Give them the 5 Ws: Who, What, Where, When, and Why. If you call them four to eight weeks before the event, you will know immediately who can attend and who cannot. Getting fifteen clients who say yes to your lunch or dinner usually means twenty-five to thirty people will attend, when you consider couples. Let them know that they are welcome to bring a guest and dinner is your treat, but it is not mandatory that they bring someone with them. One successful advisor says it this way; "Jim, you and Tracy have been great clients

over the years and I'd like to invite you to a dinner we are hosting for a small number of our local clients. You are welcome to bring a guest if you'd like and dinner will be my treat. Just let me know if you are bringing anyone besides Tracy, so that we have enough tables and food."

Your guests may also need to be reminded that this is not a product pitch, but instead a fun evening with plenty of nice people and a delicious meal. I'm suggesting that you call to invite them to your event because calling your clients saves you time, money, and the hassle of mailing invitations and waiting for replies. By the way, I have been to client-appreciation events with two hundred people but they are very impersonal and your clients will not ask questions nor will they mingle much. I have found the smaller events to be much more successful for you and a lot easier to organize. You may want to try a few smaller events and see for yourself. Calling them directly works very successfully and I know it firsthand.

6. <u>Confirm</u>: Confirm with all those who have said yes to your invitation. Send an e-mail or invitation with all the details and the 5 Ws.

Have your sales assistant call to confirm with your guests two days before the event. Some of your guests will cancel because of a scheduling conflict, but do not worry about it. It happens. Gladly invite them to the next one.

7. Arrive Early: I always like to arrive sixty to ninety minutes before the event to allow time for any surprises. Is the room set up correctly? If not, you have time to make the necessary changes. Also, check the temperature, lighting, sound, and overall comfort. Provide your personal biography or marketing page for everyone to read. (You should definitely have one of these by now.) Then meet and greet your guests, many of whom will start arriving twenty minutes before the event. Have fun and relax, because this is your dinner party (or whatever event you've organized) for them.

8. Begin the Event: Welcome everyone, share your "elevator speech," and tell them what you have planned for the evening. You should have a scripted introduction that you have rehearsed several times. This introduction should flow as easily as a conversation you have with a good friend. Know what you want to say, rehearse it aloud at least a dozen times, just like you were

there in front of your audience. Don't "wing it" ~ please don't "wing it" or else you could be very embarrassed in front of clients and their guests.

9. <u>Guest Speaker Presentation</u> (optional): The presentation should be done while your guests are eating, not after they are finished. Many folks have been up since early morning and will get sleepy after the meal. The presentation may be important but not nearly as important as your clients' enjoyment. I have watched events when a guest speaker has spoken for sixty minutes...after the coffee and dessert was served. It was a very sleepy audience. You also want a topic that your guests will find interesting or entertaining. A heavy topic like beta co-efficient or the efficient frontier will not be much fun for anyone. These folks do not care about those things, because they have you as their expert. Find a speaker who can entertain and make this evening a great success for you and your guests. A twenty-minute market over-view with some fun factoids can be completed while they eat their dinner. If you do it this way, the evening will last just about ninety minutes,

and your clients will be much more alert and upbeat.

10. <u>Close the Event</u>: Thank everyone for joining you, have a few giveaways or raffle goodies, and share a gift with the clients who have shared the most referrals with you in the past quarter or two. One advisor by the name of Jay closed the evening like this. He said, "Ladies and gentlemen, I want to thank you for joining us tonight and it looks like we've all had a lot of fun. I want to thank you for your loyalty, friendship, and your referrals. This has been one of my best years ever for referrals. As we close this dinner tonight, I'd like to share a gift with one client who has given me the most referrals in the past three months." Jay proceeded to give this client a spectacular gift basket with cheese, wine, books, golf balls and a variety of surprises, in front of the entire room. It was a fantastic sight to see. What was especially amazing is that this client, who had given Jay five referrals, was worth eight million dollars. The client was so touched by Jay's kind gesture in front of the audience that he called Jay the next morning and gave three more referrals. Public praise goes a long way in all parts of life and it

sends a message to others that you really appreciate referrals of people like them! This is an excellent way to let your clients know how much you like getting referrals!

Bonus: <u>Follow-up</u>: Send a thank-you note or an email and ask for feedback about your event. Also review what they liked and may want to hear about in the future. Review with your speaker and sales assistant as to what went well and what should be changed. Did your guests enjoy themselves? How was the speaker? Did the restaurant do as they promised? Plan the next one and have fun.

Big Bonus: <u>Other ideas for Client Events</u>:

By the way, you aren't limited to dinners or luncheons. I know many advisors who provide a short game clinic with the local golf pro, for their clients who play golf. Or try appetizers and refreshments at a local art gallery, skeet shooting, sport or fly-fishing, an afternoon barbecue, or even a Triple A baseball game. Several advisors host an event at a local movie theater on a Saturday or Sunday morning. They get a great deal with the theater because it's closed in the mornings. They choose an inspiring family movie, and then invite their clients who have children and grandchildren. Think about that for a moment. If you have interest in multi-generational planning, this type of event puts you in a very good position with the family. Be creative and do something that many clients enjoy. At my keynote presentation in Miami this week, an advisor shared a success story with me. He hosted a Valentine's Day luncheon for his widowed clients and invited them to bring a friend. It was a huge success and he gained many new clients. One advisor asked me how to find out what their clients enjoy. You can probably guess my answer. "Just ask them" I replied. When you complete the Client Profile, one of the questions you should ask your clients, as well as your prospects, are what hobbies they enjoy. Remember, your goal is to strengthen that relationship, show your clients just how much you care about their life in general and not just their money. You will be quite happy when you see the results of your efforts with these events. Have fun and be creative with these events.

# Chapter 6
# The Personal Biography Reveals Common Ground

Kimberly called Tim a week after he had met with Nick. As much as she wanted to call him sooner, she wanted to give him time to digest all he had learned. Kimberly knew that Tim would call if he was ready sooner, but she also wanted to keep the fire burning and make sure he wasn't overwhelmed.

"Tim, this is Kimberly. How are you doing?"

"Hi, Kimberly. I'm doing great, thanks to you. I've been organizing my client base and individual client profile pages and figuring out when I want to have my first client event. This has been a real 'aha' for me and, thanks to you, I have met many brilliant, nice people."

"The only clients and friends in my circle are positive, goal-oriented, encouraging, and forward-looking people. We like to believe that the future is tremendously better than the past. We also enjoy helping others who are ready and willing to make positive changes in their business and life. These are some of the things we've learned from the coaching program."

"I'd like to hear more about that program in time, but for now, I'm happy to have you as my coach. My only regret is that I didn't start working with you sooner. Having the opportunity to talk with so many experienced and successful people outside of my office has been a tremendous boost for me mentally. I've learned more about running a successful business and life management in the past month than I've learned in years here at my company with the random training programs."

"I'm so glad to hear that. Of all that you have learned in the last several weeks, is there anything that caught your attention that has gone on your project list?"

Tim paused to think about all he had learned in the past several weeks. "Actually, there is something that piques my curiosity. Nick sent his personal biography to me before our meeting. I'd never seen anyone use one of these before, except professional speakers, company officers and portfolio managers. It was like a resume, but written in a story format, which made it seem friendlier and informal. In the past, I have sent my business card and company literature whenever someone wanted to know more about me before our first appointment."

"Sure, that's what most advisors send because that's all they have. Does your company have impressive literature?"

"Yes, it looks as good as everyone else's. But, what was so intriguing to me when I read Nick's bio, was that I immediately felt like I knew him personally and had so many things in common with him. That certainly doesn't happen when I send our company literature to a prospect. Usually at the first meeting, I answer questions about what I do at my company, where I'm from, and other personal questions like that. They also want to know about our company but seem more interested in me as their prospective advisor. My instincts tell me they really want to know who the heck I am, how long have I been managing money, and what makes me different from the other hundreds of advisors in the area. I prefer not to go into lengthy detail about myself during the first appointment, because I should be asking the questions to get a better understanding of my prospects and their needs. But, if I had a personal biography to send before our meeting, it might help my prospect feel better about my personal and professional background. In your opinion, how many years should I wait before I create a bio?"

"Years? Why would you wait years to create a biography?"

"What on Earth would I put on a biography page? I've been in this business for fewer than twenty years and was in college before that. What could I write of any significance? I haven't done anything impressive yet."

Kimberly had heard this question and comment dozens of times, especially from successful salespeople. It was not only a common frustration among sales people who were in their twenties, but also from professionals in their forties and fifties.

"Tim, I'm going to guess that I am not the first person to mention to you that we are in a relationship business."

"Yes, I've been hearing that consistently from all the people I have met through you and your friends."

"Good! Then you know that the products and services you sell are commodities that people can buy from any of your competitors, through 1-800- NOLOADS, or easily on the Internet. Isn't that right?"

"Yes."

"Then why do you get any business, if there is so much competition around?"

"Many of my clients tell me they trust me know that I'm reliable and feel comfortable with me. Some are referrals from other satisfied clients."

"That's exactly it. What you sell as an advisor is not why people trust you with their money. They become clients because they're buying you, in a sense. You are the solution and the relationship that they believe will help them reach their goals, build their nest egg, and provide them with a future of good living. Would you agree?"

"Yes, they do trust me to help them accomplish these things."

"Okay, then you know they value the relationship. What are the questions you ask when you meet someone for the first time, maybe at a friend's barbecue or during a round of golf?"

"You know the regular questions: Where are you from? Where did you go to school? What do you do for a living? I'm looking for anything we have in common so we'll have some sort of connection and something to talk about."

"Tim, that's exactly the purpose a personal biography serves. The reader looks for what we refer to as common ground with the person in the bio. So, instead of you talking about yourself, the personal bio acts as an abbreviated introduction."

"Okay, I understand that and I have to ask my original question: What could I ever put in a bio? I'm only in my forties and haven't really done anything that I would consider spectacular or impressive with my life yet."

"Let's see how my memory is. Didn't you go to college in New England on a scholarship for running and compete in the Olympic Trials? Aren't you from Kohler, Wisconsin, and a competitive golfer? Tim, that's exactly the purpose a personal biography serves. The reader looks for what we refer to as 'common ground' or similar interests with the person in the bio. So, instead of you talking about yourself, the personal bio acts as an abbreviated introduction for you."

"Yes, but that has nothing to do with this business. Why would anyone care about that?" "First of all, anyone who is a graduate of that college or any other school in Boston, or is from the Boston area, immediately shares common ground with you. Anyone who plays golf knows about Kohler, Wisconsin, and probably watched the 2004 PGA Championship on TV. Finally Tim, you were in the U.S. Olympic Trials for marathon running with a personal best of 2 hours and 17 minutes. That distinguishes you from 99 percent of all salespeople, runners and Americans in the country."

"Thanks for the praise, but it was not a big thing. Many men tried out for that Olympic marathon team."

"You were in the top one-percent of all athletes in the world. Every intelligent, successful American knows that to make the Olympic team or Olympic Trials, you have to be dedicated and goal-oriented, possess incredible discipline, and have enormous drive to succeed. There's something called 'trust-transference' that creates a 'brand' in someone's mind that tells them that if someone was tremendously successful in another profession, then they are probably excellent at this profession also. The skill set you had as an athletic superstar is very similar to what it takes to succeed in this industry as well as in many other industries."

"Kimberly, I'm still not impressed with my background. Many people could have a bio that reads like mine." Kimberly had also heard this many times before, so she decided to share a story with Tim.

"I had a client who had this very discussion with me several years ago. When the topic of a personal bio was being discussed at one of my training sessions, he looked me square in the eyes and asked me what he could possibly write on his bio that had any significance. He had been an advisor for fewer than ten years. I asked him what he did before he became an advisor, and he told all of us that he was a fighter pilot in the Air Force. We were excited at the thought of flying in one of those jets. But he was flying combat missions, which put all of us in total awe. My next comment to the advisor was simple. 'You flew some of the fastest, most technologically advanced, and expensive jets on Earth, protected the United States, dealt with the stress of warfare, and came back home a survivor. Don't you think that if your prospects knew this, they would probably trust you with their million dollars to get them to their retirement goals?'

'Well, maybe, but there were lots of pilots flying these missions,' he'd replied. We could tell that he was not impressed with his past. Tim, would you trust this guy with your money?"

"I certainly would."

"Well, he originally didn't think he had anything to put on his bio either, but we helped him draft an interesting and exciting bio that attracted many affluent and successful clients. He had many military veterans and pilots as clients too, of course."

"I get it now. Maybe my background is not all that impressive to me because I've lived it. But to someone who is looking for a track record of success, I guess I probably have enough to pique their interest."

"That's it, Tim. I'm going to give you ten questions to answer about your background. When you complete the answers, please e-mail them back to me. I have a terrific writer who drafts bios within a few days. He'll make you look good, and I think you will like his style of writing. It isn't easy to write and seemingly rave about yourself, so I have outsourced this to someone who is a professional writer."

"Thanks! I'm excited to read it. I appreciate your time once again. This has been another great discussion to help my progress. Let's go for a run in a couple weeks."

Tim started to drive back to his office but stopped by the beach to think about his discussion with Kimberly. The personal bio was another simple idea that he never considered creating. But then he realized that whenever he was raving about one of his favorite portfolio managers or keynote speakers, every one of them had a bio. It was a simple way to let their clients know who they are, what their credentials are, and what they do at the firm, as well as a few personal things about them. It not only distinguished the person from any other speaker, it also positioned him or her as more successful. In a sense, it created a brand for that person.

In comparison, nobody ever learned that much about someone from a business card, that's for sure. The business card was so impersonal and just another commodity, if you took it at face value. If Tim looked at ten business cards on a table, what distinguished one from another? At least realtors took it to the personal level and added their photo, but few advisors ever did that. Tim decided right there at the beach that the bio would go to his "A" priority list and would be done within the next seven days.

Tim remembered a sales rep from one of the mutual fund companies he had met about eight years ago. The wholesaler, also known in the mutual fund industry as a regional sales rep, was one of the sharpest and most enthusiastic wholesalers he had ever met. This wholesaler had hired a business coach to review her sales practices and management of her half-billion-dollar sales territory. One of the first projects the coach asked her to complete was to answer some important questions about her interests and background. Once he had all her information, he could create a personal biography page for her. She told him that nobody in her line of business had a bio page. Well, the advantage of hiring an experienced business coach is that they know how to do things that are outside the set of habits people live within. So the wholesaler told her coach she would try it.

That bio set a standard for the wholesalers she competed against. Sales managers could read about her background, see the list of the Best Practices presentations that she could provide for their salespeople, and know specifically how she could help them increase their business. Many asked if she could teach their salespeople how to create one of these bios for them to use in their practice. Of course, most of the highly successful advisors she met with already had a bio, which further validated the importance of using one. She enjoyed implementing what other successful people did instead of following the herd. Before any appointment with a prospect these days, her personal bio is emailed to them a day or two before her meeting. Her bio has opened more conversations with excitement and interest than anything she had ever used before, because most readers looked for common interests. Remember, people tend to do business with people they like and share common interests with.

Tim reviewed some of the questions Kimberly had just emailed to his iPhone. The questions were simple enough to answer and the answers would provide a good background of anyone that took the time to answer them. It was worth a shot if it would make that much of a difference.

- Where are you from?

- What are some of your personal and business accomplishments?

- Why and how did you get into this business?

- What are your areas of expertise?

- What college did you attend?

- What sports do you enjoy playing or watching?

- List any other hobbies that you enjoy.

- Tell us about your family and where you live.

- What favorite quote tells us more about your attitude and mindset in life?

- What community involvement groups are you involved in or on the Board of?

Tim called Kimberly as he was driving to an appointment. "This biography project is going to be easy. I'm so glad you called today. You know, I don't have many people in my life who really 'wow' me, but I do have a few. You're one of them. I'm so appreciative of all you've done for me so far. Thank you."

"Tim, when I see all the progress you are making in such a short amount of time, it makes me so happy to work with you. You're a good guy and will be thrilled to reach your goal of working just four days a week, sharing more time with your family, and watching that golf handicap go to a single digit again. Working with you is such a treat for me, so I thank you!"

*Before any appointment with a prospect these days, her personal bio is emailed to them a day or two before her meeting. Her bio has opened more conversations with excitement and interest than anything she ever used before.*

## Chapter Recap

Hiring a personal coach was one of the best investments I have ever made in my life. There were many "aha" moments because one of the unknowns in life is that we don't know what we don't know. An experienced coach can help you discover more efficient ways to reach your goals, accomplish more in less time and carve out more time to enjoy in your personal life.

Take a look at most of the best athletes in the world, and you'll realize that they have a coach. So do many of the most successful sales professionals, speakers, actors and other professionals that want to succeed and compete at a higher level in their industry. Good coaches can shorten the learning curve and quickly improve your level of success. Too many of us get stuck in the mindset that we are like Superman and can do it all by yourself!

Why pay a coach when you are already successful and smart? The most important reason is because you don't know what you don't know. I invested six thousand dollars in one particular coaching program and after one year in the program, made $80,000 more than the previous year. That's a fantastic return on my investment! By the way, I was the number one sales rep in the United States at the company I worked for. I was making plenty of money and was among the top 5% of earners in this country. Making more money wasn't my top priority anymore. Working more effectively and enjoying more personal time were my two priorities.

I must admit to you that when my coach introduced me to the personal biography exercise, I did resist it. My experience was actually the foundation for this chapter. No other wholesaler or regional sales rep had a personal biography, so why should I bother? What did I really have to gain? Besides, what would I write about myself that would impress anyone? Well, the purpose of the bio is not to impress anyone. It is designed to share our background with someone who doesn't know us well or at all. The first time I used my bio was at a large sales training meeting I was conducting in Boston. The title of my presentation was *How to Strengthen Client Relationships, Gain Referrals and Grow Your Assets*, which was and still is one of the most requested presentations I give as a keynote at sales meetings. There were two hundred financial advisors and since I was new to the territory, I did not know most of them. I arrived an hour early, put a bio on each seat and got organized for the audience. The room and the seats quickly filled up and I noticed the advisors reading my bio as they sat down. Within minutes, something unusual happened. Several advisors came up to me and asked about my background. "You were in the Air Force? I was also. My uncle was stationed in Aviano, Italy." Another asked, "You run marathons? I'm training for my first Boston marathon and would enjoy talking with you about your training program." Yet another asked, "You live in Hingham? Do you play at the BlackRock Golf Course?" I told him I did and soon found out that we had friends in common. If I had only handed out business cards, this experience never would have happened. The bio opened doors and provided plenty of common ground with the audience. The meeting was a huge success and that firm did millions in business with me over the next five years. The personal bio opened the door for me.

Your action step? Create your own personal bio and you'll experience something similar to what I described. In this chapter, you have all the questions you need to answer and write about. Be sure to add personal info about yourself.

Finally, send your bio to all your clients as well as your prospects. Don't assume that your current clients know everything about you. When I sent my fresh new bio to my top 200 clients, many replied that they didn't even know I had won 2 marathons or was stationed in Italy while I was in the U.S. Air Force. Use this mailing as yet another way to keep you on the mind of your clients. One of our goals, as superstar sales professional, is to stay "top of mind" with our clients and prospects. It's another "touch" for those who are masters at keeping in touch with their clients. I'd like to hear your success stories after you share your personal biography page.

Send an email to Neil@neilwoodconsulting.com with your success stories and we can celebrate together.

# Chapter 7
# The Difference That Makes the Difference

Tim thought about Kimberly and tried to figure out what made her so unique. She was a legend among many local and national business people and considered to be among the best of the best. What was so interesting, however, was that she did not do anything that would earn her a Nobel Peace Prize or an Oscar. She simply returned all calls to her top clients and prospects within three hours, kept her promises, and usually delivered what her clients needed and earlier than they expected. What made her so unique was that many sales people over promise and under-deliver, and they are pitiful at customer service. Poor service is what many consumers have accepted as the norm.

When someone goes even slightly above and beyond the expectations, that extra mile for their clients, it "wows" the customers. Kimberly consistently wowed her clients. That was the unique recipe for success that Kimberly understood thoroughly after studying her competition. It would not take much more effort to rise above the average businessperson. So she worked just slightly more efficiently, and the results and rewards were extraordinary.

*She simply returned all calls to her top clients and prospects within three hours, kept her promises, and usually delivered what her clients needed earlier than they expected.*

Tim thought about other examples of what "just a little bit more" could result in. He thought back to his high school days in science lab. He remembered the Bunsen burner and the beaker of water that the class attempted to boil. When the thermometer in the water read 211°, the water was warm but not yet boiling. One degree more and, voila, the students had boiling water, which would create steam. Powerful train engines were run on steam. It only took one more degree of heat to produce extraordinary results. Tim realized that most of the small lessons he was learning from the professionals he met during his recent journey simply represented slight changes in his activities. He did not have to gain scores of high-net-worth clients or change his work ethic. He simply needed to make some slight changes in his activities and level of Best Practices and Practice Management. He now had many role models in his life that would gladly share the recipes for success that had helped them become multimillionaires. He welcomed better ideas. He knew plenty of others who were stubborn and told themselves that they would just figure it out on their own over time and learn from their mistakes. Of course, that was their first major mistake. It was all so clear to Tim that top achievers in most businesses will usually help a less experienced person who asks for direction and guidance. Not many people ask, however. He realized that he was different from most people. He knew that there had to be a better way and was not ashamed to ask.

Later that afternoon while Tim was out for a walk along the beach after a huge storm, he noticed thousands of mussels and quahogs that had been washed up onto the shore. Half a dozen men raced to the shoreline during low tide to collect as many of these delicious and meaty treats as they could. There were literally thousands of these fresh shellfish within an area of one hundred yards long and fifty yards wide. These guys showed up at the shore with two ten-gallon buckets each to collect these seaside treasures. Tim was stunned at how few of these shellfish they collected. Maybe it was the fresh air and the sound of the waves that opened Tim's level of awareness. Whatever the reason, he realized that there were so many opportunities for business in this country, yet so many people set such small, unexciting goals. It was like an open house at a gold mine that allowed visitors to take all the gold they wanted, yet some guy shows up with a spoon and a coffee cup because he refused to spend the money on a shovel and fifty-gallon barrel. Think BIG was the new thought on Tim's mind. That was what Kimberly's coaching program helped him do. It helped him to think big and to operate more efficiently and successfully. The days off helped refresh him for the following week. He was gradually getting his life back.

Tim remembered talking with his grandparents, who saw how hard he was working. They told him that nobody they had ever met in their nineties ever said that they wished that they had worked more hours. The regret for many of his grandparents' peers was that they did not share enough quality time with their families and friends to have more fun. He did not want to make that same mistake and he knew now that he would not.

## Chapter Recap:

What areas of your business and life can you be more productive? Most of us can be more productive with our daily schedule or preparation or daily activities.

What about you? Remember, water is warm at 211 degrees, but boils at 212!

When I went through this exercise, I noticed that I am very productive and alert from 5am until about 1, and then I hit an afternoon lag. So, I scheduled most of my important appointments or worked on projects during those peak hours. My least productive time is after 7:30pm, so that is my time to relax and get organized for the next day. Know your body clock and the peak hours for your brain.

I mentioned returning calls in this chapter because of a challenge I faced as a Regional Sales

Rep in New England. The company I was working for had an awful non-competitive group of mutual funds. Two of the twenty-five were admirable, but the remaining group was truly pitiful and lackluster. The competition I faced was outstanding. AIM and Invesco, American Funds, Putnam, MFS, Eaton Vance, Colonial, and Pioneer, had so many extraordinary mutual funds in their family that I could not compete on a product level. So, I beat my competitors on a personal service level. I returned all client or prospect calls within an hour. My voicemail stated that I would return their calls within three hours, but I made sure that I called them back within sixty minutes. I mentioned my habit of callbacks at every sales meeting, one on one meetings and every seminar I hosted. My clients knew that I was hungry for their business and willing to go the extra mile to earn it. Many of my competitors took a week to return calls from the advisors who were sending millions in business to them. That's if they returned their calls at all. They were doing so much business, that it was difficult to handle the volume of calls and requests for information. So I slowly nibbled away at their market share by going above and beyond expectations.

Advisors would complain to me about how "unappreciated" they felt when they did business with my competitors, so I used that to my advantage. I made calls every morning to thank the advisors for the business they shared the previous day. Our Daily Sales Report was posted early, so I knew exactly which advisors did business, what fund they sold and the amount. For trades less than $25,000, my internal wholesaler would call with a thank you and to see if there was anything we could do to build their business. I scripted this comment and both my internal wholesaler and I used it daily. "Your business is very important to me and I want you to know how much we appreciate it. Is there anything else I can do for you today?" Our appreciation, thank you calls and level of customer service helped me develop my territory of the six New England states into the number one territory in the US. Our clients felt appreciated, so when new assets came it, they felt loyal to send some my way, if appropriate for the client's portfolio.

The difference that makes a difference in your personal and business success may only require a slight change to create stellar results. Everything you want in life is just beyond your comfort zone! Stretch, take a chance and as always, give it your best! Brian Tracy, a best-selling sales trainer and author, gave me a great idea in 1988. He encouraged me to find other people in my line of business that were having tremendous success. Offer to treat them to dinner and ask them what they are doing differently from you. Here's a script for you to use. "If you were coaching someone that wanted to reach your level of success. What advice would you give them?"

# Chapter 8
# The Winner's Circle of Valuable Lessons and Leaders

Kimberly frequently held barbecues at her home in order to entertain friends, clients, and other business associates whose company she enjoyed. As she planned her next barbecue it occurred to her that this would be a great opportunity for Tim to make some important contacts. When she first started having these get-togethers, she sent invitations and waited for the RSVPs. Often people forgot to respond, so Kimberly dropped that idea and began calling each guest to extend the invitation. It was another way to "touch" her clients and associates. In many cases, the phone calls prompted a referral or more business from one of her associates or clients. They also developed into wonderful conversations, which often revolved around the progress made in the last twelve weeks. From a planning standpoint, she received an immediate response to her barbecue invitation and the calls worked as a way to reach out to those in her inner circle. Many of them had become friends, which made this event more like a reunion anyway.

"Hi, Tim, this is Kimberly. How are you?"

"Hi, Kimberly. Things are great here. I have been making so much progress in the last couple weeks and months that I am more excited than ever. I have more energy, need less sleep, and I'm having fun with my family again."

"That's so good to hear. I knew you would continue your pattern of success. Speaking of success, I'm hoping you can join us for my quarterly barbecue next month on the tenth. I've invited about fifty of my closest clients, associates, and friends for an afternoon of fun. They're all winners like you, with terrific attitudes. We refer to this great group as the Winner's Circle."

"Thank you. It sounds like a fun afternoon. I'll see you there."

Tim was looking forward to this barbecue and the opportunity to meet so many successful and interesting people. Good things always happened when he was in the company of fellow optimists and successful people. He always enjoyed the great chemistry and energy. Most of the other parties among neighbors were often boring to him. The evenings were filled with small talk, senseless chatter, and plenty of complaining about everything from the government to the weather. He attended these parties with his wife because she enjoyed them and he always enjoyed the time they shared together. But, if he could find an excuse to leave early, he would. This party would be different.

Many years ago, Tim attended a success seminar that featured several of the most successful people and dynamic speakers in the United States. The message he took away from the seminar that day was simple: If you want to be successful, stay around and listen to successful people, and stay away from the complainers who focus on pity parties. Spend time with people that are inspired, are inspiring, and have goals, passion, and ambition. That lesson stayed with him and was a key element for his success.

*"I've invited about fifty of my closest clients, associates, and friends for an afternoon of fun. They're all winners*

*like you, with terrific attitudes. We refer to this great group as the Winner's Circle."*

Finally, the big day arrived. Tim was so excited about the barbecue at Kimberly's house that he was as giddy as a kid around the holidays. What a great opportunity to meet so many successful people in one afternoon. It was a spectacular day with blue skies, a comfortable 80 degrees, and barely any humidity. It was just perfect, the type of day that lifted the spirit. Tim arrived at Kimberly's house around noon. She lived in a beautiful 5,000-square-foot home overlooking the ocean. It was the type of place that Tim had on his goals sheet. He'd only been there for a few minutes and was already inspired. He followed the pathway to the backyard where a dozen or so people were talking and having fun. Kimberly came right over to welcome him and made him feel right at home.

"Hi, Tim, I'm so glad to see you."

"I wouldn't miss this for anything, Kimberly. Thank you again for inviting me here to your beautiful home."

"Thank you. It's a terrific place for entertaining friends. The only ground rule while you're here is to make yourself at home. We have plenty of food, refreshments, and friendly people. I've told so many of my friends about you that you may be a bit busy meeting people today. Have fun and enjoy the day. Let me know if you need anything."

A moment later, an energetic young woman came over to meet Kimberly's new guest. "Ally, this is Tim, the fast runner and new friend I've told you about. I think you'll have plenty in common."

## *Ally's Lesson on Balance*

Ally was an Olympic figure skater in the 1970s and had won several national and world events. These days she was a TV celebrity for a national sports channel, was raising three fun and energetic children with her husband, and was doing all she could to stay fit. She was also a popular keynote speaker at many events on the coast. It was a major balancing act, but somehow Ally managed to do everything and maintain a fantastic attitude. People who watched her on television would often comment about the "spark" she had when sharing a sports story. Her passion and sincere enthusiasm were rare and quite a treat for the viewers. Many people watched that channel only to see Ally's reports. Her friends often commented to others that the Ally on television was exactly the Ally they all knew, respected, and laughed with. She was doing something she loved and it showed.

"Tim, what do you do?"

"I'm a financial advisor and really enjoy helping my clients plan for the future.

What about you, Ally?"

"I have a lot going on these days. My husband and I have three children who are very involved in sports and school events, so they keep us busy. I also work for the All American Sports Network as a producer and interviewer, which I enjoy immensely."

"Wow, how do you balance everything? Those are major time and energy commitments."

"Well, it gets challenging at times, but I've been balancing both for nearly fifteen years. The easiest way I have found to get everything done is to know exactly what I want to accomplish and

136

not waste my time on other things that might get in the way. I also make sure I stay fit. That helps my self-esteem, energy level, and confidence."

"Where do you find the time for everything?"

"I guess it comes from experience. Teamwork between my husband and me also makes a difference. There is only so much time available, so we treasure the time we share with our children while they are still young. To stay fit, I run, walk, or practice yoga daily. Exercising is easy to do early in the day before anything can throw my schedule off track. You're a runner, so you know exactly how it makes you feel. I always get more done when I've had a good workout. I have met so many people my age who look like they are fifteen years older than they are. It's scary. But what I found is that they have their habits and I have mine. Their habits usually include staying up late watching TV, drinking and eating more than they really need to, sleeping in an extra hour, and wasting several quality hours each day. Those habits may seem minor if you look at them for one day. But they sure do add up over months, years, and a lifetime. Whether the habits are good or not so good for you, they will still add up to something over the years."

Ally continued since she was on a roll now. "You're in the financial services business so let me put this in your terms. Habits are like the systematic investing programs you suggest to your clients. It may not seem like much if you look at what people contribute monthly, but it sure does add up over time, doesn't it?"

"You're right about that."

"Tim, I went to my twenty-fifth high school reunion several years ago and could not help but notice which of my classmates had habits that produced positive results, and others, awful results. I could tell with one glance which of my classmates exercised and lived a relatively healthy lifestyle. It was also painfully clear who had been living in excess. They looked terrible, barely fit into their clothes, and lacked that passion so many of us love to enjoy."

*"The easiest way I have found to get everything done is to know exactly what I want to accomplish and not waste my time on other things that might get in the way."*

Ally continued, "There's nothing wrong with having fun and enjoying a favorite beverage, but it needs to be balanced with a regular exercise program. How many pounds overweight should someone be at age forty-five? Ten, thirty, or eighty?"

"But Ally, people get busy with their jobs, families, and other commitments."

"Yes Tim, we are all busy, which makes it even more important to look at our habits, realize what they'll add up to over the years, and decide if we want that result or not. If someone weighs fifty pounds more than they did just ten or twenty years ago, it's a trend that isn't very promising as they reach middle age. I'm not saying everyone needs to run five miles a day, but the average American watches over four hours of sitcoms and news daily. Is there anything on the evening or late-night news that will make a difference in their lives? When you consider what four hours of daily television will add up to over a year, it's sixty (60) twenty-four-hour days. They spend more time zoning out on the boob tube than they do planning their retirement."

Tim was totally wrapped up in this conversation with Ally. She was mesmerizing and passionate about her beliefs and took responsibility for her life and success. She was not a victim with a case of "excusitis" who complained about being too busy with her family and work. She knew what she wanted and had the discipline to reach her goals. He also quickly did the math in his head regarding her high school reunion and realized that Ally was in her late forties. She looked like she was about thirty, however, and had the energy of a twenty-two year old. She reminded him of some of the supermodels he saw on television during the 1980s who never aged and still looked attractive and fit today. Yes, Ally talked the talk and walked the walk.

"Tim, you have an important role in our country. People are living more years than ever in history. They better have a nest egg at retirement or else they will join the rest of the masses who just never got around to planning ahead. Living a successful life requires balancing our time, efforts, health and wellness and planning ahead. Ask yourself which activities are making the best use of your time, and then put more emphasis on those things that matter the most for today and the future."

"Now I see how you balance everything, Ally. Your comments make me think of a quote I read in an article last week that posed the question; 'Is this the best use of your time right now?'"

*"Is this the best use of your time right now?"*

"That really made me think about how I've been living. When I am at work, I'm thinking that I should be at home. When I am at home, I'm thinking about all the things I have to do at work. No wonder I'm so tired, I feel like I am traveling all the time."

"Tim, we have all been there, but thanks to Kimberly and her coaching, we have all made progress over the years. You are going to meet many wonderful people today. Many of them juggle so many responsibilities, commitments, and major negotiations that my weekly routine must seem like a vacation compared to their weeks. But that doesn't matter to anyone here. We all help each other make progress when we can. There's plenty of business to go around so nobody is greedy here. I want to introduce you to one of my best friends who has taught me about the beauty of networking. Shep Becker has been a great resource for many of us here today. He's been a member and National President of the Business Networking International (BNI) for the last ten years and lives by their slogan, which is 'Givers Gain.' He does so much for so many people, yet he never asks for anything in return. Somehow, maybe out of gratitude or loyalty, we all help him when we can also. It just works out that way."

*"Habits are like the systematic investing programs you suggest to your clients. It may not seem like much if you look at what people contribute monthly, but it sure does add up over time, doesn't it!"*

As Tim thought about this, he wondered what the best use of his time was. There were plenty of activities to fill his days, but which activities brought him closer to his goals and which ones wasted his valuable time? Time is precious, yet it's wasted so often. After his conversation with Ally, Tim was ready to make major changes in his use of time.

*"Shep Becker has been a great resource for many of us here today. He's been a member of the Business Networking International (BNI) for the last twenty years*

*and lives by their slogan, which is 'Givers Gain.' He does so much for so many people, yet he never asks for anything in return. Somehow, maybe out of gratitude or loyalty, we all help him when we can also".*

## The Value of Networking and Givers Gain

"Hi Shep, how are you?"

"Hey, Ally, you were fantastic on TV last night. I enjoy your show because you always focus on the positive stories, unlike the daily news. It looked like you were having fun at the game and with the player interviews later. I have always wondered how you make your interviews so conversational when you're talking with football players who are three times your size."

"Shep, I talk to them the same way I talk to my friends. I'm sincerely interested in their thoughts, feedback, and stories. It's just like talking to our friends here today. I'm having so much fun with this sports show these days that I'd have to say these are some of the best years of my life. Shep, I want to introduce you to

Tim Swift, the new friend Kimberly told us about."

"Hi, Tim, it's a pleasure to finally meet you after all the good things I've heard."

"Thank you, Shep. It sounds like you also have a lot of fans here."

"Tim, this is an outstanding group of individuals. They're good people who believe in helping each other and expect nothing in return. It's quite unique. Many people offer help and then quickly, if not immediately, want something of equal or greater value in return. The people you'll meet here today operate, think, and behave differently. We know that in the 'Circle of Life' you get in return what you give out to others. It's commonly known as the Law of Reciprocity. It may take time, or it may happen quickly, but we don't really worry about when it happens. It just happens. There's plenty of 'good' to go around, so we all just help each other as much as we can."

"Shep, when I think of networking, I think of brokers and salespeople who hand their business card out at meetings and events with a comment like, 'If I can help you with your finances or review your statements, just give me a call.' But that isn't networking is it?"

Shep laughed heartily. "I know what you mean because I see those folks at some get-togethers and I chuckle to myself. They just don't get it. That's not networking. That's really nothing more than self-serving publicity. Nobody I've ever met really appreciates that approach, and the folks who hand out their cards wonder why their business is so bad, despite all the so-called marketing they're doing."

"I feel the same way Shep. Tell me how the best businesspeople network with others." "We simply look for an opportunity to help our peers. Great businesses are built upon referrals; you know word of mouth marketing, right?"

"Yes," replied Tim.

"Well, when we're talking to anyone who is looking for a particular product or service, we recommend our friends who can provide that service. We can recommend them enthusiastically and sincerely because we know they're good people as well as highly talented at what they do. The people looking for that service know we have high integrity and can be trusted, which are two qualities that build strong and successful businesses. As a result, the business usually goes to the friend we recommend. This helps both people and creates what we call a win-win situation that satisfies both parties. The one looking for the product or service doesn't need to waste valuable time in the yellow pages, hoping they find someone good and reliable. Our friends appreciate the business we send their way and will reciprocate when the time comes. We all care about win-win relationships here."

"You're right, Shep. When we wanted an addition put on our house, we didn't look in the yellow pages for a contractor because we don't know the quality of their work, their level of honesty, or anything about them. We asked friends and neighbors for a recommendation. One builder's name was mentioned several times. We hired him and the work was done exactly as we had planned."

"See, Tim, that's what networking is all about. We surround ourselves with others who have the core values, integrity, passion, and good-natured willingness to help others succeed."

*"The people you'll meet here today operate, think, and behave differently. We know that in the 'Circle of Life' you get in return what you give out to others."*

Shep was one of the most successful business owners on the coast. He started with nothing more than a dream twenty years ago. He volunteered to be on the board for many fund-raising groups, joined the Rotary and the Chamber of Commerce, and developed quite a reputation as a guy who kept his word. He created a sense of teamwork among the other members and set records for the fund-raisers he was involved with. Shep's favorite question to ask when he finished his project for a client was, "Is there anything else I can do for you?" He asked because he cared and really enjoyed helping people.

An interesting thing happened as a result. His customers would be so surprised by his question that they would pause for a moment, think about other people they knew who could also use Shep's expertise, and give him a referral. Better yet, they would call their friends and let them know how great, reliable, and trustworthy Shep was. A warm introduction is one of the best ways to give a referral. He received nu-

147

merous awards for his entrepreneurship and fund-raising records. Those awards were good to receive, but Shep didn't really care about that. He cared about making a difference in the community and helping others succeed and realize their dreams. He would regularly write an article in his quarterly newsletter about a local businessperson he wanted to extol. It was terrific exposure for the other business and the positive testimonial helped his clients. Yes, Shep was the master at networking because his approach was right. He wanted to help others succeed, and everything he did for others came back full circle. Shep truly was the talk of the coast, not just the town.

Tim thought about what he had just learned from Ally and Shep. This was already an enlightening afternoon, and he had only been at the barbecue for forty minutes. Something Ally said was just perfect as he prepared for his first client event. He was nervous about speaking in public to a large group of clients. But Ally gave him just the idea he needed. He'd speak to the group just as he would to a single individual, just as he was doing today. He would also watch Ally on the sports channel to see how she mastered her trade and then use some of those skills at his event. As Tim wondered what else could be in store, Shep greeted a friend of his whom he wanted Tim to meet.

*"See, Tim, that's what networking is all about. We surround ourselves with others who have the core values, integrity, passion, and good- natured willingness to help others succeed."*

# Creating An Advisory Board

"Hi, Lynn, how's life at your new beach house?"

"Oh Shep, it's great. The builder you recommended built a masterpiece for me. We love it so much that we've given his name to several of our friends who want to buy the lots close to ours."

"Thank you. You know how much we've enjoyed the home he built for us also.

Lynn, have you met Tim yet? He's been working with Kimberly this year and she invited him here to meet our friends."

"Hello, Tim."

"Tim," replied Shep, "Lynn owns her own advisory firm, which caters exclusively to the wealthiest families on the coast. They also have clients nationwide as a result of their strong referral base."

Lynn was indeed a superstar. She was selective about the clients with whom she worked. She decided to work with clients who had a minimum of two million dollars to invest, although many had much more than that. But this was not always the way she ran her book of business. When she started in the financial services business twenty years ago, she was willing to work with anyone who would open an account with her. She was constantly struggling for new accounts and doing all she could to advertise her services. She tried putting ads in the paper, attending public seminars, mailing introduction letters to the list of leads she bought each month, and even handing out business cards to anyone she met.

One day, after analyzing her business and reviewing the 80/20 Principle, she realized that her favorite and most lucrative clients were the wealthiest. They were much easier to work with and the amount of time they required was similar to the smaller accounts, but the revenue was tremendously better. Most importantly, they were more interesting, loyal, and respectful of her time. She also knew that most of her best clients were referrals from other favorite clients. Everything changed after that, including her strategy in business. She didn't feel like she was swimming upstream anymore.

"Lynn, how did you build your business so quickly?" asked Tim.

"Well, it doesn't seem like it was done all that quickly. I started the same way most advisors do. I was working more than sixty hours a week, thinking about work during the weekends, and lying awake nights worrying about problem accounts, the stock market, or some of the very negative people I had gained as clients from brokers who left the business. I was mentally and physically exhausted. But, I met a few advisors who were more successful and experienced than I was. So, I swallowed my pride and decided to ask them how they became so successful.

"I asked, If you were starting out in business today, knowing what you know now, what would you do differently?' The ideas they shared with me were common sense to them. In addition to finding and working with only clients I really enjoyed, target marketing versus mass marketing, and working more efficiently within my business, there was one idea that provided me with an 'aha' moment."

"The managing partner at our firm suggested the creation of an advisory board. He encouraged me to find five or six successful clients who were similar in personality to me, but from various career backgrounds. He suggested I meet with them quarterly over breakfast or dinner and let them be a sounding board for my business. He encouraged me to ask them what they would do if they were building a business, like I am. How would they market, how often would they contact their clients and how? What challenges did they face as they built their business? Why did they work with me instead of any other advisor? It sounded interesting but I had to ask this partner why anyone would want to spend time helping me with my business. These were busy executives."

"Lynn," my managing partner said with a smile, "successful people will always try to help another rising star. All you have to do is ask. They'll be honored."

"So I tried what he suggested and I met with each of the five clients I believed would work well together, explained what I wanted to do, and asked if they'd be a member of my advisory board. They were honored and they all said they would do all they could to help me succeed with my plan."

"How often did you meet with your advisory board?"

"We met quarterly at a terrific restaurant in a private dining room. The room gave us the quiet and privacy we needed, and paying for a dinner with five very successful people was much more productive than the ads and leads I had been paying for every month."

"How did this board help you, Lynn?"

Tim was really intrigued by this idea and wondered why nobody at his firm ever suggested it. At least he was hearing it now from Lynn.

"They taught me about strategic target marketing, what my strengths were, why they worked with me, how to eliminate things that were a waste of time, and how to stay on the minds of my better clients. For example, several of the financial advisors they had done business with in the past, contacted them two to four times a year when they had a 'hot' stock tip. As clients, they felt like they were nothing more than another commission for their broker. There was no personal relationship to speak of. To be certain that I did a better job than their previous brokers, they suggested the use of a customer relationship system that would do a better job of keeping in touch with my clients regularly.

Tim's mind was absorbing every little fact as he quickly figured how he could use this in his business.

Lynn continued, "I make the extra effort to send articles that my clients will find interesting based on their own personal hobbies or future plans. That shows them how much I personally care about them and value our relationship. When I gain a new client, I pay for a three-year subscription to a magazine that focuses on high-net-worth individuals, features articles on their needs and concerns, and offers some solutions. That magazine has created plenty of business for me, but I don't do this specifically for the business. I do this because I care about my clients and want to provide solutions for all of their needs."

Lynn went on. "The consistent message from my advisory board was how important strong relationships are to anyone's success. One of the agreements that I have with my advisory board is that we will always be honest with each other. They told me I was not in touch with them as much as I should have been which was why they suggested this automated system. We all sell similar products within the financial services industry, but the relationships we build set us apart from the competition. The affluent don't care about products. They care about solutions to their financial needs and other important life issues. I became more of a holistic financial planner. Holistic planning is the process of meeting your clients' life goals through the proper management of their resources. Life goals can include buying a home, saving for your child's education, planning for retirement, providing long-term care for their parents or leaving a legacy. Tim, those of us who build strong relationships beyond business tend to do very well. Another point my board made was that during tough, volatile markets, clients would fire their broker unless there is a strong relationship between them. I realized then, why I've gained so many wealthy clients after the recent volatility. When my clients spoke with their neighbors and peers, they praised me, according to the new clients I acquired."

"Lynn, I never thought about doing something like that. What's in it for the people who are on your board?"

"They are just like us. We enjoy helping people who want to improve their life, right?"

"Yes, we do."

"Well, my advisory board has five people who share the same philosophy. I've also helped by introducing them to successful people from other industries. If you've ever read the great classic by Napoleon Hill, *Think and Grow Rich*, then you know how important brainstorming is with a Mastermind Group. When the six of us meet for dinner, we bounce ideas off each other and create other ideas that none of us probably would have thought of if we were sitting alone. Collaborating amidst all the energy and experience creates something unique and powerful. It is truly brainstorming that goes above and beyond any experience I've ever had in the business world. Essentially, we help each other with referrals and ideas. It's the ultimate win-win relationship."

"Okay, I'm sold on the idea. How do I ask my clients if they'll be on my advisory board?"

"Simply let them know how much you respect them and enjoy working with them. Ask if they would be interested in sharing their expertise to help you build your business. Let them know that you will meet quarterly for dinner and share about two hours together. Tell them who else is in the group and how it will be mutually beneficial. Their commitment is only for one year. It's really as easy as it sounds."

"Thank you Lynn. I'm going to make the calls when I get to my office on Monday. I already know the clients I'd like to ask to be members of my advisory board."

Tim thought to himself about how simple this idea was. He had read Think and Grow Rich fifteen years ago and remembered the master-mind group idea but he didn't understand exactly how to apply it in his business. This was a perfect way to apply it and he would start on

Monday. He knew too many people who added useful ideas to their "list of things to do" but rarely got around to them. Tim did not work like that anymore. When he heard of a useful idea that would have a positive impact on something in his life, he jumped on it. Of course, that's one reason he was already so successful. His dream of working more efficiently, and maybe just four days a week, was coming closer to being a reality.

*"They taught me about strategic target marketing, what my strengths were, why they worked with me, how to eliminate things that were a waste of time, and how to stay on the mind of my better clients. I became an expert in holistic financial planning and helped my clients with more than their financial needs. "*

## The Five-Hundred Million-Dollar Man

During the latter part of the afternoon, Tim was introduced to a youthful looking guy named Doug. Tim heard several people talking about Doug's astonishing success. He had recently completed a five-hundred-million-dollar deal with a very wealthy business owner. This was the second largest deal in the history of the colossal firm he worked for. When Tim finally had a few minutes to share with Doug, he asked him about it.

"Doug, everyone who knows you at this party raves about the success you've had in your business as a financial planner. How did you gain such a large sum of money from one person? And was it really five hundred million dollars your client gave you to manage?"

"There's a long story behind that deal but I'll share it with you since you asked. This client was a prospect at one time. I kept in touch for about two years because I really felt a connection with him. I wasn't pushy and I didn't chase him, but periodically I would call to say hello or occasionally take him out to play golf. Over these two years, we developed a good chemistry and respect for each other. During this time, I was also prospecting and cold-calling like crazy. The stock market was a bit volatile and what I discovered from many of the CEOs whom I target marketed, was that they had not heard from their advisor in quite awhile. Many advisors were in the doldrums, trying to push the stock of the week but weren't selling anything. The volatility worked against them and many clients decided to watch the market before they committed more money. Because of this, many advisors stopped calling their clients. I saw that as an opportunity to prospect even more. Of course, back in the 1990s, cold calling was still allowed. The client you asked about called me out of the blue one day and said 'Doug, you need to come down to the island. I've just sold my business for a billion dollars, my stockbroker only calls when he's trying to push something, and you've been in touch with me consistently for two years, just like a good friend. We need to talk about my next move.' So, I told him I'd be there in two hours and left my office."

"What were you expecting to happen that day?"

"I wasn't exactly sure, but I had a gut feeling I'd be able to help him accomplish what he needed to do after selling his business. So we met for several hours to discuss many of his options, his goals, and what he would like to accomplish from that point on. We decided to meet again in three weeks to discuss more of the details."

"How much experience did you have with clients who have a billion dollars to invest?"

"This was my first, but I had only been in the business for ten years. That's exactly what I thought about as I made my way back home from the island. There were things that my client wanted to do with his investments that I had never experienced before. I knew I had to partner with an expert at our firm who only dealt with the super-wealthy."

*"Doug, you need to come down to the island. I've just sold my business for a billion dollars, my stockbroker only calls when he's trying to push something, and you've been in touch with me consistently for two years like a good friend and trusted advisor should. We need to talk about my next move."*

Tim was curious about Doug's thinking. "I don't know many advisors who would partner with anyone for any deal that would cause them to give up a good portion of their commission. But, you were willing to share part of your commission?"

"While driving home, I called a few of the larger producers at my office. I asked their opinion and each one said they would never bring someone in on a deal so large because they would have to give fifty percent of the commission to the other financial advisor involved in this deal. But I believed that I owed it to my client to give him the best resources we had available. Of course, I'd make much more if I did the deal myself, but it wasn't in the best interest of my client. Handling this amount of money was very complicated and I wanted to make sure it was done right."

"So, you decided to do the right thing."

"Yes, I did. I shared the details with my sales manager and asked him whom to call to help me with this deal. Two days later I was in New York City meeting the top guy at our Affluent Client Division. We worked for three months on the details of the presentation, scripted everything we needed to say, created my personal biography, and then we role-played as if we were at the actual meeting. I have never worked so hard for a deal, but this was not a deal most advisors would ever see in their lifetime. When the actual meeting happened, we were ready, well prepared, and as confident as we could be. The presentation was so successful that the client gave us five hundred million dollars to manage. There was one stipulation with this deal, however. My client gave the other five hundred million dollars to a competitor in the city and let each of us know that whoever provided a better return over the next twelve months would get the entire billion dollars. I worked so hard on this account over the next year and made sure I kept in touch and strengthened our relationship. Thirteen months later, my client closed the account with the other firm and gave us the remaining five hundred million dollars. There wasn't much of a difference in the return on the account, but I developed a much stronger relationship and did an excellent job keeping in touch as promised."

"Wow, that's incredible. As you look back on the deal, what contributed to your success?"

"My target market was and still is CEOs and CFOs, so I was comfortable with this client from day one. I also treated him as I treat my friends and focused on the relationship, not the transaction. Over time, he realized that he could trust me, that I was a good guy, and that I was competent. Those things take time to happen and develop. I'm also glad I partnered with an expert on this deal. I learned a great deal and as a result created a team of experts around me. Now I have time to do what I love to do, which is establishing relationships with the referrals I get from my best clients. I have a fantastic sales assistant and a young advisor on my team, who is awesome at extensive research and analyzing fund managers. I only have about a hundred clients, but considering their wealth, I make a terrific living. I go the extra mile with my clients and they know it because each of them has worked with other advisors in their careers, so they know how hard I work and how dedicated I am to their success. When you want referrals, it helps to have your clients speak highly and enthusiastically about you. I learned several great lessons as a result of that deal. If you ever have an opportunity like that and need advice, call me and I'll be happy to guide you along."

"Thanks, Doug, it's been a pleasure talking with you." As Tim walked away, he was thinking how generous everyone was with time, kindness, and ideas. That wasn't the environment he worked in at his office. Just then, Kimberly tapped him on the shoulder.

"Well Tim, how has your afternoon been so far?"

"This has been one of the most fascinating and enjoyable days of my life.

Please don't take this the wrong way, but I am overwhelmed by the generosity and kindness of your friends today. Are they always like this?"

"They are. Remember how I told you that I only surround myself with winners who like to help others succeed? Now you understand what I meant by that comment. Nobody here is intimidated by anyone else's success. They actually enjoy hearing more success stories. My good friend Mike Lynch once told me not to envy someone who is very successful. Just find out how they did it and apply the concept to your business. Although everyone here continues to build their business with quality referrals, they are already very successful. They don't want a thousand clients because it would dilute the level of service they provide. They build their business and wealth gradually while enjoying life at the same time."

"Ally explained it earlier as a balancing act, which made a lot of sense to me, Kimberly. I understand now."

# Chapter Recap:

Doug learned how to work hard when he was just a rookie at a major brokerage firm. He was a protégé of and tutored by the top-producing broker in the United States, who happened to work in the Boston office. Doug also followed the work ethic lessons of his father, a CEO with a dynamic personality and a passion for excellence. That's why Doug was so comfortable calling on CEOs and CFOs. What about you? What is your target market? Have you found your niche yet? You can decide to work with anyone, but you probably don't want to work with everyone. There isn't enough time, so get the biggest return on your time and effort. Some financial advisors are only comfortable targeting seniors who are ready to retire. Others focus on young executives with a promising future, while other advisors prefer to work with teachers. Find the group you are most comfortable with and become the best in the business. You'll gain plenty of referrals from existing clients, if you are excellent at what you do and if you ask for referrals as a regular habit.

When I was a regional Vice President for a New England money manager, I was coached by the amazingly brilliant, Mark Magnacca. He asked me the same question I just asked you. What is your target market? I invested time analyzing which of my clients I truly enjoyed working with and where my comfort level was. As a result, I knew I wanted to call on the top ten percent of the financial advisors in my territory, which comprised the best of the best in my region. These folks had that drive and passion like I did, so we saw eye to eye in our quest to be among the super successful. In all my years as a professional athlete and later as a successful salesman, my goal was to be among the top ten to top one percent among my peers. I loved competing with the best and still do as a professional speaker in the financial industry. Yes, wealth came with that drive, but not at the expense of our families and values.

One other lesson I want to make sure you notice in this story about my friend Doug. He knew what his capabilities were and had the confidence to partner with someone who was familiar and successful working with the most affluent people in the country. That took maturity and confidence on Doug's behalf. We all have strengths, but we also have limits to what we are capable of achieving on our own. Once again, that's why it's important to find a coach or a partner who has the experience, wisdom and expertise, to fill in those gaps and help guide us to the next level. That next level exists just beyond our comfort zone, so be smart enough to know when to ask for help.

When I decided to try to qualify for the Olympic Trials in the marathon distance (26.2 miles), I knew that I didn't have the knowledge to design a training program to help me reach my goal. I had the desire, energy, competitive spirit and drive to reach the goal, but for the most part, I just trained harder than most. When I asked George Bower, the former cross-country coach at Keene State College, if he would be willing to work with me to reach my lofty goal, he agreed. The condition was that I had to follow his carefully designed training program and learn to train "smart" not just hard. I also had to stretch for flexibility, since my hamstrings were as tight as steel cables. I agreed to both conditions and six months later, won my first marathon and averaged five minutes and twelve seconds per mile for 26.2 miles! My two hour and seventeen minute marathon, qualified me for the 1984 United States Olympic Trials. I also set a course and state record in New Hampshire, which still stands today. Without Dr. George Bower's expertise and intelligence, there is no way I could have ever run that fast. No way! Most of the runners I competed against while I trained with Dr. Bower, never accomplished much. Sure, they trained hard every single day, but they eventually burned out and never reached their potential. The moral of the story is that I want you to have the courage and brains to hire or partner with someone who has more experience and expertise than you do. The best athletes in the world have coaches to help them become even better. Know your strengths, but also know your weaker areas. Leave your ego at the door and utilize the resources and human capital that will help you achieve more than you ever could on your own.

Learn more about Holistic planning, also called Life Planning. The popularity of Holistic financial planning grew in the late 1990s and early 2000s, as the giant baby boomer generation began to think seriously about retirement. Advisors that understood this planning process asked questions that helped establish clients' core values, such as, "If you had all the money you needed, what would you do with your life?" "If something happened to the health of your parents, are you prepared to support them if they need special care?" "Do you want to leave a legacy?" The power of holistic financial planning is that it provides direction and meaning to a client's life. It allows them to understand how a financial decision affects other areas of their life. By viewing each financial decision as part of the whole, you can consider its short and long-term effects on their life goals. Here is another book you need to add to your library. *Questions Great Financial Advisors Ask* by Alan Parisse. Alan is one of the best speakers and authors in our industry and a superstar by anyone's standards. In 1990, I watched him give a presentation titled The Great Salesperson and was awed by his passion, intelligence, humor and delivery. If you want to learn from a superstar, Alan is one of those people you want to Google.

# Chapter 9
# Partnering With Those Who Add Value

"Partner with the best and ten minutes for the rest."

"Tim, let me introduce you to my friend Jay Irving. He lives a couple hours away, so it's always a treat to see him. Ten years ago, Jay left the firm that he was working for because he wanted to be more independent. His peers told him he was taking a huge risk leaving the major Wall Street firm, but that firm focused on transactions and hundreds of cold calls every week. That was not the way Jay wanted to run his business. He now generates over a million dollars in commissions each year and is happier than he ever dreamed of."

Jay and Tim spoke for thirty minutes about client events and how to partner with several sales reps that are very important to them. Tim's office manager had an open-door policy for the mutual fund and annuity sales reps, because they would buy breakfast or lunch and supply him with golf balls. So each day in the office, there was a constant parade of reps, also known as wholesalers, sharing their favorite fund ideas to anyone who would listen. Most of these folks wasted an enormous amount of the advisors' time because they habitually dropped by the branch for what was referred to as a "walk-through" rather than making an appointment. They talked to any advisor who would give them time and waited by the office doors of those who were on the phone.

"Tim, when I first started in this business, I would take calls and visits from all the sales reps that were also referred to as wholesalers of the various fund companies. I never liked being rejected when I prospected, so I didn't want to reject them either. But after a few years, I looked at the silly trinkets they handed out and was bothered by the fact that each one told me that their products were the best. Only a few of these reps really understood my business and could share effective business building ideas with me. One of Kimberly's friends suggested a solution that I liked so much, I implemented immediately.

Whenever a sales rep called me for an appointment, I would politely ask them what was unique about their product and how they could help me grow my business. If they offered a compelling idea, I would schedule a ten-minute appointment to hear what they had to say. If I was impressed and felt a good connection with them, then we would meet again for a longer period of time. I told them I worked by appointment only, because I was busy running my business. If their ideas were not unique, I would tell them I only work with the five sales reps that add real value to my practice. I developed strong partnerships with the best wholesalers in our business and we succeeded together. That simple suggestion helped me stay focused while I was in the office and gave me a lot more time to be with my family, go fishing, or play golf."

"So, in essence you've partnered with a team of experts from a handful of mutual fund and annuity companies, that share stories and ideas from other successful advisors? What was their reaction to your stance of working by appointment only?"

"The best sales reps also worked by appointment because they were busy managing their territory. They ran their business just like I ran mine, so they didn't have time to walk around offices looking for anyone who would talk to them. They targeted their market and developed partnerships exactly like we do with our clients."

Once again, Tim learned a simple solution to an issue that affected his business and his personal life. He could not believe how sheltered he had been at his firm. Nobody in the office ever shared the ideas that he learned about during this great afternoon at Kimberly's home. He realized that sometime in the near future, he had to find a better environment to work in and a better firm to work for.

*"I only work with the five sales reps that add real value to my practice. I developed strong partnerships with the best sales reps in our business and we succeeded together."*

## Chapter Recap:

Once again, I want to use a quote that you have previously read in this book. "Is this the Best use of your time, right now?" There are so many distractions these days, that it takes quite an effort to stay focused on those projects that are most meaningful. Blocking out the distractions, help us make progress towards the successful completion of the most important projects on your list. If you are a financial advisor or in sales in another industry, I encourage you to partner with those representatives that are excellent at what they do and are willing to share ideas to help you increase your business. I had two nicknames when I was a sales rep calling on financial advisors. Mr. Value Add and Mr. Win Win. I always had my clients' best interest in mind and was constantly keeping up with best practices, so that I could help them be more successful. The Law of Reciprocity proved true each time. The more I gave, the more I gained. Our relationship was an absolute Win Win. The same philosophy and behavior holds true in a relationship with a romantic partner. Sharing kindness, positive energy, always wanting the best for each other and doing all you can to add a smile to their lips, adds to the emotional bank account and often a strong relationship.

# Chapter 10
# If You Don't Like Something ~ Change It!

Tim left the barbecue feeling like a new man. He promised himself that he would keep in touch with his new circle of friends because they were such a terrific resource for him and their enthusiasm was such a boost. He also wanted to create strategic alliances with several of them so he could send referrals their way. This day with the Winner's Circle was the jump-start he needed, to get out of the rut he was in. He was determined and ready to make a big decision. He sensed that something was about to change and opportunities would be coming his way. He thought about the lessons he had learned and decided to implement three new steps into his practice each quarter. It would bring him closer to his goal of running a successful and efficient practice, while enjoying plenty of leisure time with his family and friends. Some of the changes in his business could be done quickly, while others, such as scheduling client events, would take more planning time. It was all progress toward his ultimate goals.

*Tim thought about the lessons he had learned and decided to implement three new steps into his practice each quarter.*

Despite the positive changes Tim made in his business, his office manager's daily focus on commissions, revenue, cold calls, wholesaler visits, and the product of the month, did not satisfy him anymore. His manager was still stuck in the work philosophy of the 1980s, because that was the only method of doing business he knew. Tim's work with Kimberly had taught him that he was not a victim, so he started searching for a better company to work for.

He registered with Join A Firm to see if he could find a work environment that was more conducive to his style. Within two weeks, something wonderful happened. Kimberly called one of her clients and told him about Tim. Her client, Ryan Shanks, is the CEO of Finetooth Consulting. His company helps financial advisors find a better "fit" for employment with other advisory firms looking for talented advisors. Ryan plays the role of a Sports Agent for advisors, like Tom Cruise played in the movie, Jerry Maguire. Their consultative approach and style of work blended perfectly with Tim's, so when they met for lunch, the chemistry was ideal.

Ryan asked Tim to describe the ideal work environment he envisioned. They talked for more than two hours and by the end of lunch, Ryan knew of three companies that would be a perfect fit for Tim. Within days, meetings were set and six weeks later, Tim was offered a tremendous opportunity with a Registered Investment Advisor in the next town. The new company offered a lucrative profit-sharing program and paid bonuses each quarter based on client satisfaction. Of course it was important to add new clients but the focus was more on quality than quantity. The happier and more satisfied the clients were with his attentiveness, solutions, and level of contact, the better he did. Tim became an expert at "Life Planning" for his clients who were transitioning from the accumulation stage to the retirement stage of their lives. Clients trusted him with all of their financial needs such as estate planning, wills, long-term care, college funding, and various insurance needs. They also trusted him with wealthy referrals that wanted more than just a financial advisor. When a prospect or a referral asked Tim what he offered as an advisor compared to the competition, he would confidently ask the important "life" questions that Mark had taught him months earlier. Before he would agree to take on a new client, he wanted to learn about their values, goals, fears, and dreams first. He wanted to know that keeps them awake at night, instead of leading with products. This holistic approach captured clients from the competition every month.

*Tim became an expert at life planning for his clients who were transitioning from the accumulation stage to the retirement stage of their lives.*

The clients appreciated the newsletters, which discussed quality of life issues, concerns on growing older, raising positive children and fun things to do with grandchildren. They also appreciated the birthday and anniversary cards that Tim personalized through the Send Out Cards Company. It was very clear to the clients that Tim and his company sincerely cared about them and their families. The company's website focused on building communities and providing scholarships and funds to the areas they did business in. Tim found this appealing and refreshing compared to his last company. He finally found the perfect environment for him.

## Chapter Recap:

Most of my years in sales and as a professional athlete involved plenty of hard work as you would expect, and probably know from your own experience. I will admit that I was definitely a Type A personality and a workaholic. In 2000, I learned how to work smarter and that was the beginning of a life change for me. These positive changes inspired me to write this chapter. Most competitive and driven people have a list of projects that could fill several pages. You can't accomplish everything all at once and if you try, you'll drive yourself bonkers and be constantly frustrated. Nothing is ever enough and you search for the elusive perfection, which by the way, does not exist. Decide on the three most important projects and focus on those for the next twelve weeks. Stay focused, measure your progress and if you finish all three within the next three months, then work on three more. At the end of the year, you'll have successfully completed twelve large and important projects that will make a difference in your career or home life. Remember one of the best secrets to success is that we measure progress, not perfection.

Years ago, I attended a seminar hosted by Jim Rohn. He was quite a master of quotes during his life and at this seminar; one of his quotes that I'll remember forever was this one. "If you don't like something change it. You aren't a tree" At the time, I was working for a company I wasn't very proud or fond of. Hearing that quote was just the nudge I needed to call a few executive recruiters. It's always interesting when you decide to take action, toss your dreams into the universe and quickly realize there are opportunities just waiting for you. All you had to do was seek! Some say that's a coincidence but I believe we manifest these things into our life. Within six weeks of contacting the executive recruiters, I was working for the best company in my career. I still feel that way as I reflect back fourteen years later. I'm so glad I made that change!

If you are ready to make some positive changes in your life, have the courage to take the next step. If it doesn't work out the way you planned, you can always go back to what you were doing. But I believe you can find better opportunities and you'll never look back! Life's too short to be unhappy at work or in a relationship that no longer satisfies you. By the way, life is also too long to endure such misery. Go ahead and create a masterpiece of your life. As my sweet daughter said to me one day during a beach walk and a challenge to jump into the waves when the water was just forty degrees, "YOLO Dad ~ You only live once!"

*As my sweet daughter said to me one day during a beach walk and a challenge to jump into the waves when the water was just forty degrees, "YOLO Dad ~ You only live once!"*

# Chapter 11
# Working Smarter Provides A Balanced Life

Tim received an invitation to Kimberly's next barbecue and remembered a conversation he had with Jeb Bashaw during the first barbecue. Jeb (JB) explained how he had built a very successful full-service financial advisory practice by providing outstanding service and developing meaningful client relationships. He built a reputation of being their "go-to" guy. He strengthened those relationships by hosting a variety of monthly client events. He knew his clients had various interests and hobbies, so each month was a different event, designed specifically for the clients who had interests in that area. This was an ideal opportunity to show his appreciation and for his clients to get to know each other, since many lived within forty miles of his office. There were wine tastings, meeting and talking with local artists at an art gallery, and private dinners for twenty or thirty clients at a time. He also added skeet shooting, hunting at a local hunting club, a night at the local AAA baseball game, a carnival day for the kids, fly-fishing at a private lake, a short game lesson with the golf pro at his country club, as well as many other things that appealed to various clients. Jeb and his team knew what their clients enjoyed because part of their consultative approach involved asking about their hobbies and interests. It wasn't a surprise to anyone that Barron's chose him as the #1 Wealth Manager in Texas this year.

Jeb cares about his clients like he cares about his family, and he's a role model husband and father for sure! His clients know how much he cares and how he wants to be the primary contact for any needs they have. His strategic alliances cover every need any client could possibly have. He has alliances with experts who handle mortgages, financing for high-end automobiles, private jet time-shares, vacation rentals in the US and Europe, and the list goes on and on. His clients know that he's just one phone call away. The client events always provide plenty of fun and strengthen the relationship with the clients and their friends. Many clients ask if they can bring a friend or a couple to the event. Jeb always welcomes his clients to bring friends, because they have even more fun. Quite often, the guests become referrals and eventually clients, because after meeting Jeb, they realize how much he cares about his clients. Showing appreciation for their business and referrals, showed how much Jeb cared about the long-term relationship. Tim quickly realized that if it worked that well for JB, then it would probably be just as successful for his company.

*Not all clients had similar interests, so each month was a different venue, designed specifically for the clients who had interests in that hobby or area of enjoyment.*

Tim had his event coordinator organize monthly client events including a family afternoon at the movie theater, golf outings, private dinners, outings at the local sports fields, Fourth of July barbecues, holiday open houses, and anything else he thought would be fun. The list of monthly events for the upcoming year was included in his Happy New Year card. All the dates and details were printed on large postcard that most clients kept by their calendar or posted on the refrigerator. Quite often, the calendar of events was posted next to the family photo from Tim's previous events. The photo cost just three dollars to produce, but it was worth plenty because it kept Tim's name and photo in clear view every day at his clients' homes or offices.

The last firm he worked for, held one big client event toward the end of the year. It was at an upscale museum that could almost comfortably hold the eight hundred clients who attended. It was impersonal, expensive, and a nightmare to organize. Holding a conversation with the small percentage of his clients who attended was impossible. On the contrary, Tim's events seemed special, more intimate and fun. When Tim and his wife were invited to various functions, they had more fun at the smaller events with fifty or fewer guests. Since Tim's clients were more like him and his wife, it made sense to follow the same formula. The events he hosted had a maximum of fifty people, which included clients and another couple, if they decided to bring two friends. What a simple way to show gratitude to the clients who made his life so fulfilling.

Tim's top clients received at least a dozen "touches" each year. Some of the touches were his phone calls, and he also sent a birthday and anniversary card. Usually a program like this took hours every month to coordinate, but the office manager paid for a system that was automated. They simply outsourced it to a company with the expertise and solid reputation of an automated customer-relationship management system. It was the Send Out Cards system that Lynn had been using successfully. Tim's clients raved about him because they knew he had their best interests in mind.

The four-day workweek became a plan that Tim embraced with a smile! He worked four-day weeks like every other advisor in the office. The team that supported the office handled all the important, non-revenue-producing matters. Each team had its own unique skill set. The president of the company explained to Tim that it was a matter of putting the right players in the right position. That made their high level of customer service and contact so much easier to accomplish. Administrative people do not want to sell anything or give presentations. Salespeople do not like to get bogged down with administrative duties. Both are important to their customers however, so putting the right people in those positions is the most productive and satisfying use of time. Each member of the team had their unique abilities that contributed to the success of the company. It worked flawlessly.

For the first time in his career, Tim had a life. His relationships at home improved and he even started coaching his daughter's soccer team. He and his wife enjoyed a three-day vacation at least every six weeks, in addition to semi-annual vacations with the entire family. He continued to exercise regularly of course, and had more energy than he had in years, because he wasn't at work seven days a week anymore. Work was fun again and he loved the new company! Life was good. Heck, it was all good! And it all happened because Tim took action. He didn't whine and moan or have a pity party. He had himself to thank and as the Beatle's song says ~ "We get by with a little help from our friends."

Tim still attended Kimberly's barbecue each year and everyone from that group attended his semiannual feasts. The members of the network supported each other and continued to add more winners with great attitudes. Tim often stopped to think of how much progress he had made in the past eighteen months. He would be forever grateful to his good friend Kimberly, who had introduced him to people who cared about the success of others and who truly believed in win-win relationships. Many years ago, Mr. Zig Ziglar said something at a seminar that continued to make a difference in Tim's life. "You can get everything you want in life, if you help enough other people get what they want."

Mark Magnacca taught him how to create a brand for himself and how to present more effectively. There were a few more lessons Tim learned from Mark over the next year. He finally discovered how effective an "elevator speech" could be, when he had to describe what he did for a living. It took some work and practice, but when Tim was asked what he did for a living, he simply mentioned that he helps his clients build and protect their wealth and then helps transfer that wealth to the clients' heirs. As a result, Tim's clients refer to him as their "personal CFO," which is quite a compliment. He also learned how to script his presentations for the best impact and clarity for his clients and referrals. It was quite a remarkable, memorable year of tremendous progress. The small steps of progress had added up to a marathon of results.

Tim's wife surprised him by hiring a local golf pro to help him with his golf game. Within a year, his handicap was in the single digits again. He golfed with clients on Fridays and his family on weekend afternoons. Life was so good again. He was no longer a workaholic. The stress levels were much lower, his relationships were better than ever, he had about one hundred loyal clients, and he was making more money than he ever dreamed of. This success came as a result of working with a coach, favorable introductions to other successful people, being open-minded to work smarter and taking responsibility to make changes in his life. All of this was the result of being ready to make changes. When Tim came home at four o'clock one afternoon to watch his daughter's soccer game, he realized something that he had not noticed in a long time. His passion was back. He was feeling the runner's high again in everything he was doing. This was exactly the goal he had set with Kimberly a year ago and achieving it was worth all the time and effort he had applied. He was "in the zone" again.

*The stress levels were nonexistent, his relationship with his family was better than ever, he had about one hundred loyal clients, and he was making more money than he ever expected. Golfing consistently again was the icing on the cake. This success came as a result of working with a coach, favorable introductions to other successful people, being open-minded to work smarter and taking responsibility to make changes in his life.*

Tim realized through all of these experiences that things in life can change quickly if we know exactly what we want, are willing to work to make it happen, and if we partner with the resources we need in order to accomplish our goals. He was so thankful to live in the greatest country in the world, where the opportunities are endless. He was well aware that people from other countries come to the United States because it's known as the land of opportunity. He had never heard anyone say; "Gee, if I could just move to India, China, Brazil, or Malaysia, I could really be successful." He understood that it does not matter what rut someone is in, because there are plenty of solutions if that person has the desire to improve his or her life. In the investment business, one quote that is splashed throughout the industry is "past performance is no guarantee of future results." Another famous quote along the same concept states that 'the past does not predict the future.'

*"Past performance is no guarantee of future results and the past does NOT predict the future!"*

The same philosophy applies to life. It does not matter what we have experienced in our past. Maybe we grew up poor, came from a broken home or a dysfunctional family, ruined some good relationships, or failed in business several times. Those experiences can be used as lessons, as painful as they may be, but they do not predict the future. We cannot change the past, but our future is our responsibility. By the way, it's estimated that 85% of all families have some sort of dysfunction, so move on. Remember, the past does NOT predict the future.

During Tim's morning run, he thought about his talk with Colonel Tom Kirk at Kimberly's barbecue. Colonel Kirk was a fighter pilot in Vietnam and was shot down during a bombing mission. He was captured and lived in a prison camp for five agonizing years that were filled with torture. The miserable experiences he endured were unimaginable to most human beings. What impressed Tim, however, was the Colonel's great attitude. He remembered Colonel Tom's comments about surviving tough times and how we all have tough times in our lives. The challenges we faced in the past are lessons in life. We cannot change the past, so we need to learn lessons from it, leave it where it belongs and move on. Don't let the lessons be roadblocks in your future. Use them as stepping-stones to make the present and future more successful.

Tim vividly remembered Colonel Tom's words of wisdom. "Our future is in our hands. We live in the greatest country in the world with no limits on what we can do or the amount of money we can make. Do all you can to help other people succeed in life and reach their goals and you will enjoy a very successful life. You are responsible for your future." Colonel Kirk was one of the most successful financial advisors and real estate developers in Vail, which was no surprise to anyone who knew him. He sincerely cared about the success of others and absolutely loved life. He was unlike anyone Tim had ever met. He was in his late seventies and still loved to ski more than one hundred days a year. He also entertained the locals by playing his saxophone three nights a week in the downtown nightspots. That's living life with passion, and that was exactly the future Tim wanted.

*"Our future is in our hands, Tim. We live in the greatest country in the world with no limits on what we can do or the amount of money we can make. Do all you can to help other people succeed in life and reach their goals, and you will enjoy a very successful life. You are responsible for your future."*

Whenever they spoke on the phone, Colonel Kirk often reminded Tim that our future is in our control. "Stay focused on your future while enjoying today. Read the great books available from other successful people and surround yourself with winners. Take a good look at your habits and ask yourself if they are bringing you closer to your goals or farther away from them. And be sure to share a lot of time with your kids. Before you know it, they're grown and gone."

The more Tim thought about Colonel Tom's advice, the more he thought about the audio series he listened to from Tony Robbins, the world famous motivational and transformational speaker. He said if there is something you have talked about doing for several years or many months, try it. Don't let the pessimists and losers ever talk you out of your dreams and goals. When someone gives you advice, consider the source.

*"Stay focused on your future while enjoying today. Read the great books available from other successful people and surround yourself with winners. Take a good look at your habits and ask yourself if they are bringing you closer to your goals or farther away from them. And be sure to share a lot of time with your kids, Tim. Before you know it, they're grown and gone."*

# Chapter 12
# Going the Extra Mile in Life and Business

As the years went on, Tim collected quite a library of inspirational books. The more Tim read and learned from the network of superstars he associated with, the more he thought of the "extra mile." There are no crowds in the extra mile. When he read or heard about top salespeople or athletes being at the peak of their game, he recognized that as the extra mile zone. Tim was a bit amused to notice that it did not take a tremendous amount of extra energy or effort to succeed. One of the main reasons many people were not as successful as they could be was because they had a habit of giving up too easily. If they had just tried a little bit more, they would have found the "vein of gold."

Take a look at the difference in time or scores between the gold medalists and fourth place finishers in the Olympics. The difference is negligible. Look at the golf scores after a major golf tournament. Quite often, the difference between first place and second or top five is a stroke or two. But the reward is tremendous! First place wins a million dollars or more, and the others win considerably less. First place averages out to be a quarter of a stroke better each of the four days. That's all! Look at the championship horse races and you'll often see a similar result when a horse wins by a nose. The payouts are vastly different between first and fifth place, yet the horse and jockey won by a few inches. Realize that you don't have to be tremendously better than your competition and it's easy to improve your skills by a few percentage points, if you want to. Go that extra mile with your family, in your career and if you compete as an athlete.

Those people in the extra mile mentality climb past the masses, work intelligently, strategically, and rigorously to accomplish their own personal mission, and now compete among the top 10, 5, or 1 percent in their field of work. Of course, they do not rest on their laurels, because they know that if they aren't making progress, then they are probably falling behind. Most folks are not willing to do that "little extra" to be among the best of the best, but that's okay. Some people will take the path of least resistance while others want to squeeze every last drop of achievement and fun out of life. The lessons Tim had learned about going the extra mile inspired him about the future.

# Chapter 13
# Who Is Tim Swift?

I know Tim's story extremely well on a very personal level because it is an amalgam of me and many of the interesting and successful people whom I have met in my life. I am so fortunate to have met and learned lessons from the wonderful people you have read about in this book. The last thirty years of my life and career have been quite an interesting journey and I expect the next thirty to be even better.

The reason I have written this book, however, is because I want to help people rediscover the fun they once had in their business and life. Remember the passion and excitement we had when we first started in our business? It was like being in love for the first time. Prospecting and gaining new clients was exciting. Seminars and client events in the evening were things we looked forward to. We were on a mission and life was good! But after many years, many clients, and multiple changes in the industry, a number of us became overwhelmed, tired, and overworked. The fun seemed to disappear and we were far less passionate than we were in the beginning. Going to work was not as exciting and prospecting was not one of our favorite activities anymore. Maybe it does not happen to everyone, but I know many people who have experienced it, including myself.

I had raised a billion dollars in mutual fund sales and was determined to be everything to every client, which eventually became an impossible task. I was desperate to find a better way to balance my life and share quality time with my family. Fortunately, I found a business coach who helped me reduce the distractions, hassles, and the size of my client base. He also helped me rediscover the fun again. I want to help you find the fun and fall in love with life and your career again. I hope everyone who reads this book will realize that the difference between good and very successful is simply the result of a few small positive habits that multiply exponentially to produce success. Please notice that I did not suggest you work harder, but I do encourage you to work smarter. Life is short, so let's have some fun as we make progress in life.

Your call to action is to decide which changes you can make in your business and life during the next ninety days. What does your ideal month look like? How much money is enough? If you had three months to live, what would you do differently? What "messes" would you like to eliminate from your life? Thirty years from now, as you reflect on your life, will you look back at these days with pride, or regret? What will you be the most proud of? I encourage you to take action now because the sooner you do, the better you will feel. Are there changes you have thought about for three years but have not had time to do them? If you do not make the changes, how are you going to feel three years from now? Remember the words from Colonel Tom Kirk. Our future is our responsibility, despite what our past comprises. Focus on those activities and actions that you have control over. Attitude, passion, energy level, fitness, partnering with others for mutual success, and making the best out of most situations you find yourself in are just a few of those things we do have control over.

Make the best of all the rest. If you don't like what you are doing or the company you work with, then have the courage to change matters. Like many of us who have made positive changes in our life, you'll wonder why you didn't do it sooner. Just don't carry those thoughts for long, because maybe the timing wasn't just right then, as it is now.

# Chapter 14
# Resources To Help You Remain Positive and Encouraged

We all need a boost now and then, right? The final chapter in this book includes resources to help you make progress, remain positive, and keep things in perspective. Follow your dreams. Do something you love. Personal growth is mandatory but suffering is optional.

*"Fortunately, I found a business coach who helped me reduce the distractions, hassles, and the size of my client base. He also helped me rediscover the fun in my life and business again. I want to help you find the fun and fall in love with life and your career again."*

The following are some of my favorite sayings and quotes that have helped boost my spirits when I needed it. We become what we think about most, and these are some of the best readings for positive thinking that I have found over the past thirty years.

# **Daily Reading to Stay Positive**

Nothing in This World Can Take the Place of Persistence!

Talent will not;

Nothing is more common than unsuccessful people with talent.

Genius will not; Unrewarded genius is almost a proverb.

Education will not; the world is full of educated derelicts.

Persistence and determination alone are omnipotent!

The slogan "press on" has always solved the problems of the human race!

~ Calvin Coolidge

# Expect to Succeed

If you think you are beaten, you are; if you
think you dare not, you don't;
If you'd like to win, but you think you can't, it's
almost a cinch you won't.
If you think you'll lose, you're lost.
If you think you are outclassed, you are.
For in this world we find...
SUCCESS begins with a fellow's will. It's all in
the state of mind.
You've got to think high to rise,
You've got to be sure of yourself before you
can ever win the prize.
Life's battles don't always go to
The stronger or the faster person,
But sooner or later, the one who wins
Is the one who thinks they can!

(Source: Think and Grow Rich by Napoleon Hill,
published in 1937)

# The Optimist Creed

Promise Yourself...

To be so strong that nothing can disturb your peace of mind.

To talk health, happiness and prosperity to every person you meet.

To make all your friends feel that there is something special in them.

To look at the sunny side of everything and make your optimism come true.

To think only of the best, to work only for the best and to expect only the best.

To be just as enthusiastic about the success of others as you are about your own.

To forget the mistakes of the past and press on to the greater achievements of the future.

To wear a cheerful countenance at all times and give every living creature you meet with a smile.

To give so much time to the improvement of yourself that you have no time to criticize others.

To be too large for worry, too noble for anger, too strong for fear, and too happy to permit the presence of trouble.

# IF by Rudyard Kipling

If you can keep your head when all about you
are losing theirs and blaming it on you,
If you can trust yourself when all men doubt
you but make allowance for their doubting too,
If you can wait and not be tired by waiting, or
being lied about, don't deal in lies, or being hat-
ed, don't give way to hating, and yet don't look
too good, nor talk too wise:
If you can dream—and not make dreams your
master, if you can think—and not make
thoughts your aim;
If you can meet with Triumph and Disaster and
treat those two impostors just the same;
If you can bear to hear the truth you've spoken
twisted by knaves to make a trap for fools, or
watch the things you gave your life to, broken,
and stoop and build 'em up with worn- out
tools:
If you can make one heap of all your winnings
and risk it on one turn of pitch-and-toss, and
lose, and start again at your beginnings and
never breathe a word about your loss;
If you can force your heart and nerve and sinew
to serve your turn long after they are gone, and
so hold on when there is nothing in you Except
the Will which says to them: "Hold on!"
If you can talk with crowds and keep your vir-
tue, or walk with kings—nor lose the common

touch, if neither foes nor loving friends can
hurt you; if all men count with you, but none
too much, if you can fill the unforgiving minute
with sixty seconds' worth of distance run,
Yours is the Earth and everything that's in it,
And which is more, you'll be a Man, my son!

# Don't Quit by Edgar A. Guest

When things go wrong, as they sometimes will, when the road you're trudging seems all uphill, when the funds are low and the debts are high, and you want to smile but you have to sigh, when care is pressing you down a bit—rest if you must, but don't you quit.

Life is queer with its twists and turns. As every one of us sometimes learns. And many a fellow turns about when he might have won had he stuck it out.

Don't give up though the pace seems slow— you may succeed with another blow.

Often the goal is nearer than it seems to a faint and faltering man; often the struggler has given up when he might have captured the victor's cup; and he learned too late when the night came down, how close he was to the golden crown.

Success is failure turned inside out—the silver tint of the clouds of doubt, and when you never can tell how close you are, it may be near when it seems afar; so stick to the fight when you're hardest hit—it's when things seem worst, you must not quit.

## Favorite Books and Audio Programs

- Customer Centered Selling by Rob Jolles
- Think and Grow Rich by Napoleon Hill
- The Magic of Thinking Big by David J. Schwartz, PhD
- Unstoppable by Cynthia Kersey
- You Can if You Think You Can and The Power of Positive Thinking by Dr. Norman Vincent Peale
- Unlimited Power by Anthony Robbins
- The Product Is You and SO WHAT by Mark Magnacca
- StorySelling for Financial Advisors by Scott West and Mitch Anthony
- Clients for Life by Mitch Anthony
- Questions Great Financial Advisors Ask by Alan Parisse
- Inspire Any Audience by Tony Jeary
- See You at the Top by Zig Ziglar (Also listen to GOALS)
- The Psychology of Success by Brian Tracy
- Golf Is Not a Game of Perfect by Dr. Bob Rotella

## **Useful Resources**

- www.nightingale.com This website for the Nightingale Conant company provides an excellent catalog of audio programs, books, and learning resources to educate yourself while traveling by car, plane, bicycle, or train. Like many of you who will read this book, I still enjoy going to an exciting motivational seminar and getting fired up. The audio programs available at Nightingale Conant will help you keep that fire burning.

- Horsesmouth.com is a terrific website for financial advisors and other salespeople. You'll receive ideas every day on Best Practices and numerous success stories from other very successful people in our industry.

## Focus on the Positives Daily

Think about how you feel as you watch the evening news or read the local news- paper. It's filled with gloom, doom, and people behaving ignorantly. Many years ago, I started a bedtime routine with our children to help them focus on the positives each day. I did it because our oldest son was waking up in a terrible mood every morning. He was six years old so I knew he did not have much to be concerned about compared to working adults. When I asked him at bedtime what was on his mind, he quickly rattled off all these negative experiences he had during the day. He had gotten into a disagreement with his best friend, lost a toy, and even fallen down and cut his knee. These were the last thoughts on his mind before bed.

Fortunately, I have read books on positive attitude and success since I was a young teenager and realized that I had to change the mental tape in his young mind. I asked him what the best part of his day was and he immediately broke into a huge smile as he told me about all the fun things he did during the day. His mom took him to the zoo and heard a lion roar, saw a rhinoceros and an anteater, as well as a gigantic giraffe. He was beaming and went to bed in a very happy mood. He also woke up in a wonderful mood. We did this every night and watched his attitude change. One night, our four-year-old son looked at me and asked, "Dad, what about the best part of my day?" He had been listening to me ask his brother each night and wanted to be involved in the fun conversation. We have been doing this for six years now. If you want to raise happy children, ask them about the best part and be sure to use those specific words, because if you just ask people how their day was, the response is often just a single word like fine or okay. I share that story as a father but also as a businessperson. We are all working hard to help our clients succeed, but occasionally we meet a client who is constantly negative and irritating. You can waste so much time dwelling on that one pessimist OR you can focus on those clients that appreciate what you do for them. Please do yourself a favor since you deserve it. Focus on the good you do and the people you have helped. If you do have a client that many people would call Mr. Cranky and he is driving you whacky, give him to another advisor or even to a competitor. Usually, a client like that is nasty to everyone. Life is just too short and you do not deserve to be treated like that. Focus on your positive accomplishments each day, week, and month. We know the daily news focuses on the most horrible items, daily, so just out of curiosity, note all the positives and see how you feel after that.

IF you are on Facebook, feel welcome to enjoy my daily positive quotes on **Neil Wood's Optimist Island Daily Quotes**. I often share these quotes on **LinkedIn** also. Feel welcome to connect with me on both websites. www.linkedin.com/in/neilwoodconsulting/

# Positive Self-Talk

How much time does the average person spend in the morning making himself or herself look good before heading out the door? When I have asked that question during a seminar, the typical answer is approximately forty-five minutes. I have also heard six minutes but cannot imagine the hygiene issues there! Let's say it takes about forty-five minutes for showering, washing, brushing hair, picking an outfit that we feel really confident in, and then heading out the door. Here's one more question for you? How much time does the typical person invest in positive self-talk so that they can feel just as good on the inside as he or she looks on the outside? The answer ranges between just a few minutes and none at all. Isn't that surprising?

Positive self-esteem and confidence, powerful visualizations, and thoughts about our successes are so helpful in reaching our optimal levels of performance. Successful actors, athletes, musicians, and businesspeople know just how important this is. They see themselves succeeding as if they were watching a movie in their mind.

If you are doing this already, then you know what it does for you. If you are not, then it is one of those things that you may consider starting in the near future, as in today. Be a cheerleader to yourself. On a pad of paper, write all the positives you can about yourself. Do all you can every day to protect and boost your confidence. We become what we think about most. Please understand this small but powerful fact. **Our thoughts are like muscles. The ones we exercise the longest, become the strongest. Be careful what you say to yourself because your mind and body are definitely listening.**

# Chapter 15
# Neil Wood's Personal Biography

Neil Wood has a unique combination of success as a professional athlete as well as a sales rep within the investment industry. He joined the U.S. Air Force in 1976 for a four year assignment to Aviano, Italy. While enjoying his duties, which required Top Secret Clearance, he learned about two activities that fascinated him; running for the peace of mind and investing in mutual funds for a healthier future and retirement. Thirty-eight years later, Neil is still passionate about both!

During the early 1980s, Neil raced in marathons as a professional athlete. He qualified for the U.S. Olympic Trials in 1984 with his marathon time of 2 hours and 17 minutes, while winning his first marathon. That time still stands as the New Hampshire state record today. He's raced and won championships throughout the Mediterranean countries and in the United States as well.

The 1980s is also when Neil decided to apply his habits of discipline, positive focus, persistence and goal setting to a career in the financial services industry. His passion and sincere enthusiasm continues today. Neil travels throughout the United States providing Keynote presentations and training seminars, primarily for but certainly not limited to salespeople in the financial services industry. Over the last twenty-five years, Neil has worked with top achievers in a variety of fields. The common denominator that he has found among the most successful achievers is very simple to reproduce. They have made small positive changes in their habits, daily activities and attitudes, which have produced exponential changes in their results.

Neil lives in Massachusetts, in his dream home on the ocean. He loves sharing time with his three enthusiastic children, photography of sunsets and sunrises and sharing time with friends. If you would like to share your success stories, please go to Neil's website: Neil Wood Consulting. He is also the co-author of Dating Success After 40, which was written with Nancy Michaels. They believe that online dating involves sales and marketing and they have shared dozens of tips to help you market yourself effectively if you are participating in the online dating sites.

## For Worldwide Speaking Engagements:
### Neil@NeilWoodConsulting.com
### 781 264-3361

Made in the USA
San Bernardino, CA
06 March 2018